BORN AGAIN

DECONSTRUCTION OF THE DIALOGUE BETWEEN NICODEMUS AND JESUS

A PHILOSOPHER NAMED JESUS

Jose A. Alegria-Morales

© 2025 Jose A. Alegria-Morales.
BORN AGAIN
jose.alegria.morales@icloud.com
All rights reserved. The reproduction of this work in whole or in part, its incorporation into a computer system, or its transmission in any form or by any means (electronic, mechanical, photocopying, recording, or otherwise) is prohibited without the prior written permission of the copyright holder. Failure to comply with these rights may constitute a criminal offense under the intellectual property legislation.

The content of this work is the responsibility of the author and does not necessarily reflect the views of the publisher. The author is responsible for the content of the text.

Published by: Jose A. Alegria-Morales
ISBN eBook: 979-8-9986206-6-9
ISBN Paperback: 979-8-9986206-7-6

Content

PREFACE	1
INTRODUCTION	3
EXEGESIS Nicodemus and Jesus	6
Night Dialogue	6
Nicodemus	7
Place of the Meeting	8
Historical Context	9
Riot in the Temple	14
Nicodemus' ruse	16
Jesus Born Again	19
Nicodemus Misunderstood	20
Born of the Spirit	21
Epiphany in the Desert	23
Kingdom of God	26
Everyone	37
Will of the Wind	40
Synthesis	43
HERMENEUTICS Echoes of Jesus	45
Cultural Hegemony	45
Philosophical Parallels	49
Baruch Spinoza (1632-1677)	49
Immanuel Kant (1724-1804)	52
Karl Marx (1818-1883)	56
Friedrich Nietzsche (1844-1900)	65
Antonio Gramsci (1891-1937)	71

- Martin Heidegger (1889-1976) 75
- Michel Foucault (1926-1984) 80
- Synthesis 84
- RETURN TO GOD 86
  - The Concept 86
  - Socio-Theological Criticism 88
  - Praxis 91
- A PHILOSOPHER Called Jesus 96
  - His Philosophy 96
  - Revolutionary Content 97
  - Distortion of his Message 99
  - Synopsis 103
- POEM Epiphany in the Desert 105
- PARABLE A Truncate Enterprise 107
- EPILOGUE 110
- REFERENCES 112

DEDICATION

This work is dedicated to those fortunate ones who, in a flash of lucidity, achieved the remarkable transformation known as «Born Again». People who are courageous enough to see a new horizon and to transform their existence, aligning their steps with the light of their newly intuited worldview, woven into the mystery of their new life.

ACKNOWLEDGMENTS

I would like to express my deepest gratitude to Sophy Rivera Lanzot for the opportunity to share a reflection at the Prayer Circle of the Presbyterian Church in Hato Rey, San Juan, Puerto Rico. On that occasion, I presented a detailed analysis of the dialogue between Nicodemus and Jesus, as recorded in chapter 3 of the Gospel of John. This analysis drew on exegetical and hermeneutical approaches to provide a comprehensive interpretation of the text. The experience described, characterized by its remarkable enrichment, constituted the principal source of inspiration for the writing of this literary work.

I would like to express my most sincere gratitude to my wife, Olga J. Rivera-Pacheco, for her meticulous critical reading and her recommendations, which proved invaluable for this literary exposition.

I would like to express my most sincere gratitude to the developers of artificial intelligence, DeepSeek® and Gemini®, for their invaluable collaboration. The first helped me establish the logical sequence of the paragraphs, while the second contributed constructive suggestions, that enriched the content of this work.

PREFACE

«Who is not born again cannot see the Kingdom of God.»

This enigmatic and forceful statement motivated the development of this research. The statement is located in the night dialogue between Nicodemus and Jesus of Nazareth, which can be found exclusively in chapter 3, verses 1 to 21, of the Gospel according to John. This passage is notable for its profound philosophical content, making it one of the most significant dialogues in the Gospels.

The expression «Born Again» encompasses a profound spiritual truth that, throughout generations, has intrigued, inspired, and challenged believers and scholars alike. Despite its apparent symbolic simplicity, fundamental questions arise that demand deep and systematic reflection.

The objective of this research is to unravel the meaning of the concept «Born Again». To this end, we have conducted a thorough analysis of the various interpretations and meanings attributed to it, examining whether it should be understood as a metaphorical symbol, a specific ecclesiastical ritual, a purely personal transformation, or even a transcendental «spiritual rebirth».

In parallel, an analysis is conducted of the relationship between the expression «Born Again» and the concept of the «Kingdom of God». This concept has been the subject of numerous interpretations and debates throughout history. The objective of this study is to examine whether this «Kingdom» constitutes a future eschatological reality, a heavenly place, a divine manifestation in the world, or a state of collective consciousness. In this context, the question arises to whether it is essential to experience a profound spiritual transformation to gain a comprehensive and profound understanding of the complex and surprising nature of the «Kingdom of God».

Throughout this analysis, we have attempted to avoid dogmatic speculation. In contrast, we have approached this topic with intellectual honesty, and methodological rigour, from a revelatory perspective that seeks to distinguish the philosophical core from later theological constructs and religious myths. In this study, readers will find a thorough and well-researched analysis of a key passage from the Gospel of John, which expounds on the fundamental elements of Jesus of Nazareth's complex social philosophy.

The study's findings provide an enlightening perspective on the impact of spiritual transformation on achieving optimal human potential. The readers are invited to undertake a rigorous analysis that promises to broaden their understanding of these philosophical and spiritual foundations.

> *Jesus said, «Let him who seeks to continue seeking until he finds. When he finds, he will become troubled. When he becomes troubled, he will be astonished, and he will rule over the All.» (As quoted in the second proverb of the Gospel according to Thomas).*

Jose A. Alegria-Morales
jose.alegria.morales@icloud.com

INTRODUCTION

In the Gospel of John, chapter 3, we encounter one of the most enigmatic and profound dialogues in Christian tradition: the nocturnal encounter between Jesus of Nazareth and Nicodemus, a Pharisee leader. Historically, this passage has been interpreted almost exclusively through a theological lens, focusing on concepts of salvation and individual faith. However, this book proposes a radically different reinterpretation. By removing the dogmatic elements, we can reveal a consistent and revolutionary philosophy that not only challenged the social order of its time, but also has surprising resonance with the foundations of modern and contemporary thought.

To unravel this hidden philosophy, our investigation will unfold in two interconnected stages: the exegesis of the original text and its subsequent philosophical hermeneutics. In this process, we will explore how the figure of Jesus can be understood not only as a Jewish messiah, but also as a thinker whose ideas on personal autonomy, freedom, and social justice anticipated the giants of Western philosophy.

The initial segment of this analysis constitutes a **philosophical exegesis** of the dialogue between Jesus and Nicodemus. Our objective is to extend beyond literal interpretation and contextualize Jesus's words to identify the fundamental principles of his great social philosophy. By carefully analyzing each phrase and metaphor, we will reveal the philosophical elements that, in our understanding, constitute a call to individual and social transformation:

Introduction — Born Again

- ❖ **The concept of «born again»**: A profound transformation of being.

- ❖ **The allegory of the «will of the wind»**: The concept is presented as a metaphor for an invisible and uncontrollable force that drives the «reborn» to achieve the freedom and assertiveness of the wind.

- ❖ **The symbol of "darkness in the night"**: A contrast between the authentic life of the light and the inauthentic existence of the shadow, where hypocrisy and injustice are bred.

- ❖ **The metaphor of the «Kingdom of God»**: A model of social order that aims to manifest justice and the fullness of life on Earth.

- ❖ **The «Return to God»**: A concept that presents death as a return to the origin of our existence, as well as the process of our relationship with God before birth, during childhood and adulthood, and at the moment of death.

The purpose of this stage is to establish the philosophical framework for Jesus's thought, providing a solid frame of reference for subsequent analysis.

Following the identification of the philosophical core of the dialogue, the second stage will focus on **comparative hermeneutics**. This section of the book establishes a critical dialogue between Jesus's ideas and those of certain modern and contemporary philosophers who have shaped our understanding of existence of being and society.

Through a rigorous exercise in parallelism, we will demonstrate how Jesus's concepts have their equivalents in the thought of the following authors:

- ❖ **Baruch Spinoza**: The life impulse of his «conatus» and the search for freedom from the «slavery of the passions».

- ❖ **Immanuel Kant**: The universal moral law of his «categorical imperative».

- ❖ **Karl Marx**: The driving force of social change in his «historical materialism» and the vision of a seemingly utopian «communism».

- ❖ **Friedrich Nietzsche**: The autonomy and self-improvement of the «Übermensch» (a term generally translated as «superman») versus «herd morality».

- ❖ **Antonio Gramsci**: The struggle against «cultural hegemony» and the role of «organic intellectuals».

- ❖ **Martin Heidegger**: The overcoming of «Dasein» (human being) as «Das Man» («inauthentic being») through the awareness of «finitude» (inexorable death).

- ❖ **Michel Foucault**: «Self-care» as a tool of resistance against social power structures that produce «docile bodies» by imposing their rules.

Upon completion of this thought-provoking journey, readers will realize that Jesus's philosophy is not a relic of the past. Instead, it remains a powerful voice that still resonates strongly with the most pressing issues of our time, such as authenticity, freedom, justice, and the nature of true human and social transformation.

A warm welcome to our esteemed readers!

EXEGESIS
NICODEMUS AND JESUS

Night Dialogue

The concept of «Born Again» originates in the Gospel of John (Chapter 3), during a significant night-time encounter between Nicodemus, of conservative-leaning Jewish religious leader, and Jesus of Nazareth, a Jewish leader with revolutionary tendencies.

> *John 3:1-8*: There was a Pharisee named Nicodemus who was a ruler of the Jews. This man approached Jesus **at night**.
>
> **Nicodemus said to Jesus**, «Rabbi, we know that God has sent you to teach us because no one could perform these miracles unless God were with he.»
>
> **Jesus replied to Nicodemus**, «Truly I assure you, unless someone is born again, he cannot see the Kingdom of God.»
>
> **Nicodemus asked Jesus**, «How can anyone be born again when they are old?" Can he enter his mother's womb a second time and be born again?»
>
> **Jesus replied to Nicodemus**, «Truly I tell you, unless someone is born of the Spirit, he cannot enter the Kingdom of God. What is born of the flesh is flesh, and what is born of the Spirit is spirit.»
>
> **Jesus added**: «Do not be surprised if I tell you that everyone must be born again.»
>
> **Jesus concluded his dialogue with Nicodemus by sentencing**, «The wind blows wherever it wishes. You hear its sound, but you do not know where it comes from or where it goes. So is everyone who is born of the Spirit.»

Nicodemus

Nicodemus was a notable figure. While the Gospel of John identifies him as a Pharisee, historical data on his sociopolitical status suggests that he belonged to the Sadducee group. He was regarded as "principal among the Jews" and held a distinguished position in the Sanhedrin, the highest religious and political authority in first-century Judaism.

> **Sanhedrin:** *This was the supreme council (that is, the Supreme Court) that interpreted and applied Jewish law according to the Torah. This group, composed of seventy-one members, including the High Priest and prominent figures in Judea, wielded significant religious and political authority, even gaining recognition from Rome. During Jesus's time this recognition reflected its significant impact on the political and religious spheres of the Jewish life.*

Given his role as member of the Sanhedrin, it is reasonable to conclude that Nicodemus was a prominent figure in Judea's political elite. This position would have required him to be a staunch defender of the religious order established by the Torah Law and a guardian of the political status quo. His influence, wealth, and privileges were closely tied to the effective management of the Temple and the delicate balance of power within the Roman system.

A social disorder or revolt against Rome jeopardized not only the authority of his sociopolitical class, but also the very survival of the Temple and its institutions, including the Sanhedrin. By cooperating with the imperial authorities, he maintained a degree of autonomy and avoided more severe repression, which could have resulted in the loss of his privileges and the suppression of Jewish practices. Nicodemus embodied the characteristics of a conservative leader, demonstrating a commitment to containing any revolutionary threat and safeguarding the established order.

Consequently, Nicodemus was not expected to consider being «born again», much less to offer and demonstrate broad support to Jesus of Nazareth. Doing so would entail giving up his extensive social privileges, which would be a great loss for him.

Place of the Meeting

The Gospel of John (chapter 3) recounts the dialogue between Nicodemus and Jesus without specifying its exact location in Judea, mentioning only that Nicodemus approached Jesus **"at night"**. However, the historical context allows us to infer the most likely scenario.

Members of the Sanhedrin, including Nicodemus, primarily resided in Jerusalem, as this was the seat of the institution: the **Hall of Hewn Stones** (*Lishkat Ha-Gazit* in Hebrew), located within the Temple complex. This space served as the nerve center of Jewish power, where the Sanhedrin interpreted '*Halakha*' (Jewish Law), resolved judicial cases, and exercised its civil and religious authority.

According to the account in John 2, the meeting occurred shortly after Jesus expelled the merchants from the Temple. This fact suggests that the conversation took place in or near Jerusalem. Although the text does not explicitly state it, Nicodemus' habitual residence and the centrality of the Temple in the city —where even figures such as Caiaphas and Annas held Sanhedrin meetings in their own homes— support this conclusion.

Jerusalem was undoubtedly the most dangerous setting for Jesus of Nazareth to discuss the «Kingdom of God», especially in regard to individuals such as Nicodemus. The timing of the intervention, which was conducted during nighttime hours, was meticulously planned to take advantage of the darkness as a strategic asset. This approach was intended to discreetly conceal both the actions and intentions of the Sanhedrin's agent.

The city of Jerusalem was of significant religious importance, being the spiritual center of Judaism and the site of the Sanhedrin, an entity that wielded great influence in the Jewish community. Jesus's teachings on the «Kingdom of God» in Judea were seen as a threat by the religious authorities and the established interpretation of the Law. In Jerusalem, this preaching became a subversive and dangerous act. Furthermore, his recent revolt in the Temple had intensified tensions, creating an atmosphere of growing hostility towards his figure.

The undercover agent uses the the darkness of night as camouflage.

Historical Context

Nicodemus and Jesus both lived in a time of constant wars for the conquest of territories and the plundering of their resources. Judea was in a constant state of instability, where the Roman government was always on the lookout for any signs of rebellion that might challenge its military dominance.

In this context, the Sanhedrin, as the Jewish authority, had two functions: to ensure compliance with the Torah (Mosaic Law) and to prevent conspiracies against Rome. The threat of the Zealots, insurgent groups that attacked both Roman soldiers and collaborating Jews, exacerbated the climate of violence and mistrust.

The fact that Nicodemus sought Jesus **at night**, just after Jesus had expelled the merchants from the Temple by force, reveals multiple meanings. On the one hand, it reflects his desire for a deep and reserved dialogue. On the other hand, it demonstrates the necessary caution in the face of the growing friction between Jesus's movement and the established religious authorities.

Thus, this meeting was about far more than just a friendly conversation. It was the intersection of two distinct visions in the turbulent context of Roman Judea during the Messianic Era. They were two people who belonged to distinct and antagonistic social classes.

Nicodemus, a wealthy Orthodox Jew and prominent member of the Sanhedrin, embodied the religious-political establishment. His political power was dependent on constant servile negotiation with the Roman imperial power. His wealth and status were proof of his pragmatism. He served the interests of the Sadducees in Jerusalem while cultivating loyalties with Rome, the true power behind the throne.

Jesus of Nazareth was an itinerant Rabbi who traveled throughout Judea preaching a revolutionary message that denounced the socio-economic injustices of his time, challenging the structures of religious and political power. In a historical context marked by rulers eager to expand their dominions to exploit other people's resources, he proposed a radical alternative: the construction of a society based on social justice. His vision included leadership exercised by humble people, dedicated to serving the most disadvantaged within a framework of peace, love, and mutual collaboration, even with foreign nations.

The geographical context amplified the tension between the social positions of Nicodemus and Jesus of Nazareth. The Roman province of Judea encompassed key territories (Judea, Samaria, Perea, and Galilee), each with its own ethnic and religious particularities. It is clear that in this mosaic of cultures, Jesus's message from Galilee took on a particularly disruptive character for the established order in Jerusalem.

It was a time when Jewish spiritual life in Jesus's time was articulated around two fundamental pillars.

1. **The Written Law (Torah):** It is centered on the official teachings imparted by the priests in the Second Temple in Jerusalem and in the synagogues. This corpus, composed of the Pentateuch (Mosaic Law), was consolidated during the Babylonian exile and serves as the unshakable doctrinal foundation of Judaism.

2. **The Oral Tradition:** It was upheld by itinerant teachers and independent rabbis who interpreted and adapted the Mosaic Law to new social contexts. These teachings, transmitted in public spaces and plazas, offered a more dynamic application of religious precepts to everyday realities.

The Pharisees were the main exponents of this oral tradition. They transformed the streets and squares into open classrooms. Their oral debates and interpretations revolved around the application of the Torah, from ritual to all aspects of social life. They followed the example of the scribes of the Babylonian captivity. They sought to preserve Jewish identity. They did this at the cost of strict separatism (apartheid). This separatism was focused on ritual and ethnic purity. This tradition was not a static and silent set of texts; it was a body of teachings, discussions, and jurisprudence that was passed down from generation to generation through teachers (rabbis) and their disciples.

First-century Judea was a political and theological hotbed where conflicting social factions such as the Sadducees, Pharisees, Zealots, and Essenes coexisted. In this environment, a teacher's authority depended not only on his erudition but also on the public perception that he reflected the characteristics of the long-awaited Messiah.

> **Messiah or Christ**: In Hebrew, it is transliterated as Mashiach. In Greek, it is transliterated as Christos. This figure was created by Jewish priests during the Babylonian captivity. It represents the ideal future leader who will bring peace, justice, restoration, and redemption to the Jewish people. This leader will lead them toward political liberation and, eventually, domination over the rest of humanity.

In addition to the itinerant preaching of the Pharisees, there was that of the Essenes. It is clear that despite sharing the realm of teaching and public preaching, the messages of the two sects were radically different. The Essenes promoted a re-evaluation of the dominant religious culture, emphasizing the urgent need for change. This made them revolutionary figures and, therefore, ideal candidates to be considered the Messiah. The Essenes sect featured John the Baptist and Jesus of Nazareth.

John the Baptist proclaimed a message of radical repentance, linking baptism to the forgiveness of sins and announcing the imminence of the «Kingdom of God». His asceticism and prophetic tone firmly place him in the lineage of the prophets who emerged in the wake of the Babylonian captivity. John's worldview was not just a set of religious beliefs; it was a philosophy of life based on personal honesty and social integrity.

Jesus of Nazareth, on the other hand, taught with an authority that surprised his listeners: «As one who had authority, and not as the scribes and Pharisees» (Matthew 7:29). He not only interpreted the Torah, but often transcended or deepened it, saying things like, «You have heard that it was said... but I say to you...» (Matthew 5:21-48). This generated both admiration and rejection because it challenged some of the interpretations and emphases of the oral tradition.

The period of Jesus was marked by a lively intellectual debate covering theology, ethics, and politics. Interpretations of the Mosaic Law and oral tradition generated intense controversies, while under Roman rule, the political question remained latent, fueling the messianic hope of liberation. In this context, disruptive voices emerged. These voices questioned established post-Babylonian Judaism.

In this context, the dialogue between Nicodemus and Jesus was more than a theological exchange; it symbolized the clash between two worldviews. On one side was the established religious structure that negotiated its privileges with the Roman power. On the other, there was a resounding call for a «spiritual rebirth». This new vision boldly reshaped human relationships based on divine principles, roundly rejecting all forms of oppression and social injustice.

Riot in the Temple

Before meeting with Nicodemus, Jesus went to the Temple in Jerusalem, the headquarters of the Sanhedrin.

> *John 2:13-16: The Jewish Passover was near, so Jesus went up to Jerusalem.*
>
> *In the temple, he saw people selling oxen, sheep, and doves, and he also saw the money changers sitting there.*
>
> *He made a whip out of cords and drove everyone out of the temple with their sheep and oxen.*
>
> *He also poured out the money changers' coins and overturned the tables.*
>
> *He commanded those selling doves, "Get these things out of here! Stop turning my Father's house into a marketplace!"*

From the perspective of the members of the Sanhedrin, Jesus of Nazareth's actions in the Temple must have been viewed as a blatant challenge to their authority and the established order. They must have been viewed it as a deliberate act of subversion and rebellion.

The Sanhedrin was made up of a select group of chief priests, scribes, and elders, including Nicodemus. This judicial body administered and supervised Temple activities. Merchants and money changers were an accepted and regulated presence, as their activities facilitated worship. They provided animals for sacrifices and exchanged foreign coins for those acceptable in the Temple. Jesus boldly challenged the authority of those who permitted and benefited from them by disrupting and disorganizing these operations.

The Temple was, without question, a place of immense religious significance for the Jewish community, especially during the celebration of Passover. It is evident that Jesus's actions, in overturning tables and expelling the people, would have generated considerable chaos and a significant disruption to religious activities. This action was undoubtedly disrespectful to a sacred place and a threat to social order.

Jesus was clearly assuming an authority that only the members of the Sanhedrin possessed. These individuals saw themselves as the guardians of the Law and the Temple. Jesus's interference, particularly with force, was an encroachment on their prerogatives.

During the Roman occupation, any act of popular unrest or uprising was considered sedition. Jesus's actions in the Temple constituted a clear threat to the stability and relations of the Sanhedrin with the Roman authorities, and could have sparked a revolt. Beyond the obvious violation of established norms, Jesus's actions were a veiled criticism of the commercialization of worship and the corruption that had infiltrated the Temple, turning it into a profane place. This criticism would have been perceived as highly offensive by those who benefited from the system.

In short, the members of the Sanhedrin undoubtedly interpreted Jesus's actions as a grave act of insubordination, a disruption of the established order, a blasphemy against the Temple by profaning its "normality", and a potential threat to their authority and the political and religious stability of Jerusalem and Judea. Jesus's actions in the Temple were a clear protest, a rite of purification, and a revolutionary act. This action, combined with the growing support from the Jewish community, was the catalyst for the Sanhedrin's decision to seek a way to arrest Jesus and bring him to criminal trial.

*The Temple riot:
protest, purification and revolution
in a single act.*

Nicodemus' ruse

The Gospel of John clearly states that after the Temple riot, Jesus of Nazareth received a visit from a member of the Sanhedrin named Nicodemus during the night. It is crucial to understand that, despite their shared Jewish background, Nicodemus and Jesus embodied diametrically opposed sociopolitical positions. It's clear that Nicodemus's visit after the Temple riot was no coincidence. It is clear that Nicodemus was investigating the man who claimed to have the power to disrupt Temple activities during the celebration of the Jewish Passover.

Nicodemus began his dialogue with Jesus diplomatically, certain that this would win his receptivity and reveal his messianic identity. The dialogue began by acknowledging him as a «wise Rabbi, come from God», which, at first glance, denoted respect and profound admiration.

> **Nicodemus said to Jesus**, *«Rabbi, we know that God has sent you to teach us because no one could perform these miracles unless God were with he.»*

It is important to note that a prominent member of the Jewish community, a member of the Sanhedrin, addressed Jesus, giving him the title of «Rabbi» and stating that God had sent him to «teach us». This Jesus, who had recently caused a disturbance by disrupting order in the Temple of Jerusalem, was now recognized by a member of the Sanhedrin as God's messenger to impart teachings to the entire Judean society. Nicodemus knew that Jesus's teachings were not intended only for a select group. They were meant for all the inhabitants of Judea. This included the most disadvantaged and marginalized classes. It also included the highest echelons, including members of the Jewish elite like himself.

Nicodemus did not limit himself to praising Jesus's wisdom but also recognized other outstanding qualities in him. He made it clear that his miracles were a demonstration of divine power granted by God. In the current context, Jesus performed feats that defied convention, such as healing illnesses where medical professionals had failed, exceeding all expectations. Consequently, throughout history, the supreme wisdom of the universe, interpreted as a divine entity, has been considered to grant divine support to Jesus.

Nicodemus recognized in Jesus an exceptionality that transcended the merely human, perceiving in him a distinction and superiority in knowledge and authority.

However, as a member of the Sanhedrin and the ruling elite, he was concerned about the political impact of Jesus of Nazareth's teachings and actions.

Therefore, Nicodemus' statements, as a representative of the Jewish elite, pursued a dual purpose. On the one hand, they expressed his admiration for someone who stood out among the other Rabbis and scribes who traveled throughout Judea teaching about the Mosaic Law and political and social issues. On the other hand, he sought to have Jesus's answers reveal the truth about his messianic identity, that is, his intentions in the political sphere.

If we grant Nicodemus the benefit of the doubt, it's clear that, despite his admiration for Jesus, he chose to play it safe, fearing the loss of his privileged status under Sadducee and Roman rule. Therefore, his support for Jesus was expressed through discreet words and gestures, exclusively during that single nocturnal encounter carefully isolated from prying public eyes.

However, a more thorough analysis of his behavior undoubtedly leads us to a more critical interpretation. Clearly, Nicodemus tried to manipulate Jesus that night, given his prominent position as a leading member of the Sanhedrin, the Supreme Court of Justice. His objective was clear: gain Jesus's trust to fulfill the mission entrusted to him by the Sanhedrin after the Temple revolt. Although Nicodemus failed to discern Jesus's political intentions, it's evident that he decided to warn the Sanhedrin about the threat Jesus posed to their privileges in the face of Rome after Jesus's enigmatic responses. After his conversation with Jesus, Nicodemus must have told the Sanhedrin, «Jesus is a brilliant man, but he will cause serious social disorder and jeopardize our our privileges». This warning led to Jesus's arrest, trial, and condemnation under Roman law.

> *Beware of the flatterer;*
> *his flattery is a weapon*
> *to dominate you,*
> *not to honor you.*

Jesus Born Again

Faced with Nicodemus's ruse, Jesus skillfully evaded the purpose of the argument, leading to a radical change of subject. Jesus confidently responds to Nicodemus's inquiry about his supernatural abilities through an allegory.

> **Jesus replied to Nicodemus,** «Truly I assure you, unless someone is born again, he cannot see the Kingdom of God.»

In his response to Nicodemus, it is evident that Jesus was referring to himself, as his words came as a reply to Nicodemus' observations had made about him. It is clear from what Jesus said that his authority, wisdom, and ability to perform miracles came from being «born again». This «spiritual rebirth» granted him the freedom and wisdom necessary to perceive and understand the «Kingdom of God» in all its magnitude and breadth. In short, true freedom and true wisdom (that is, Logos) emanate from the depths of our own being when we achieve and maintain a profound connection with God.

Jesus made it clear with this statement that he experienced a «spiritual rebirth». This means that before his «spiritual rebirth», he was just another man, bound by the customs and traditions of his society. This spiritual transformation was necessary to transcend the paradigms of his time, develop a critical perspective on his surroundings, and achieve a profound understanding of the truth. In other words, it is about having had a direct connection with the Logos.

> **Logos**: *This term comes directly from Greek philosophy. It refers to a divine intelligence that permeates the universe and leads toward the knowledge of absolute truth. The Logos manifests itself in human beings in the form of intuition, generally as a result of meditation, argumentation, discourse, or teaching.*

After achieving divine communion with the Logos, Jesus made a decision that would define the rest of his life: to fight with all his strength, mind, and soul for the restoration and universal expansion of the «Kingdom of God». In order to fulfill this vital mission, it is crucial to combat the social structures of power. These structures are the root cause of the world's social problems because they keep citizens ignorant (in sin) and distance them from the Logos. In this context, social power structures are akin to the devil.

> **This is precisely why
> I came into the world:
> to undo what the devil has done.**
> 1 Juan 3:8

Nicodemus Misunderstood

Nicodemus, besides being surprised by Jesus's response, did not immediately understand the meaning of the metaphor of «born again» as it was initially presented to him.

> *Nicodemus asked Jesus*, «How can anyone be born again when he is old?. Can he enter his mother's womb a second time and be born?»

His question is a clear example of a literal interpretation of Jesus's words, demonstrating a fundamental misunderstanding of the spiritual significance of the expression. As a teacher of the Written Law, he was used to literal interpretations and a system of rules and traditions. The concept of a «new spiritual birth», which involves a radical internal spiritual transformation, represented a radically different concept from his life experience.

Nicodemus' worldview did not require change, as his privileged socioeconomic position made him certain that the knowledge he had acquired throughout his life represented not only his reality, but also the optimal possible one. Given this positive perception of himself, his question denoted confusion and an inability to conceive of a renascence that was not physical.

Born of the Spirit

Jesus explained to Nicodemus that being «born again» meant experiencing a «spiritual rebirth». This is essential to seeing, understanding, and accessing the «Kingdom of God». What originates in the human species is inherently human; what emanates from the spirit is spiritual.

> **Jesus replied to Nicodemus**, «Truly I tell you, unless someone is born of the Spirit, he cannot enter the Kingdom of God. Whatever is born of the flesh is flesh; whatever is born of the Spirit is spirit.»

The expression «born again» refers to a **profound transformation of being**, a metanoia, or change of mind and spirit. This step represents more than a simple improvement or adjustment; it is a reconfiguration of perception and understanding on both the individual and social levels.

> *Metanoia: Transliterated in Greek as metanoien, it refers to a profound and transformative change of mindset, a conversion, or a shift in perspective. It involves a review of beliefs, attitudes, and ways of understanding the world, leading to spiritual, emotional, and intellectual renewal. It is a process of internal reflection that results in a new way of thinking and acting.*

Those who experience a «spiritual rebirth» become, in essence, their own parents and guardians. They assume absolute control over their existence, thoughts, and actions, developing a critical and reflective outlook on themselves and the world around them. This «rebirth» is not an instantaneous transformation; it is an intimate and progressive process of inner evolution.

However, such a metamorphosis inevitably faces challenges, particularly in societies that resist any deviation from the established order. In Judea during Jesus's time, the authorities imposed a rigid political and cultural uniformity and demanded unconditional submission to the religious order. Any dissent was labeled as sedition.

What was the moment and circumstances in which Jesus experienced the spiritual transformation he called «born again»? Born and raised in Nazareth, Galilee, he distinguished himself as a skilled contractor in the construction industry after his adolescence. He specialized in handling materials such as wood and stone, a trade instilled in him by his adoptive father, Joseph.

> For you know the grace of our Lord Jesus Christ: <u>Though he was rich, for your sake he became poor</u>, so that by his poverty you might become rich. (2 Corinthians 8:9 [Underline added]).

His distinguished professional career placed him among the wealthy Jewish figures of his time, likely associated with the Pharisee circle due to his socioeconomic status. However, his keen intelligence led him to transcend established dogmas. He listened to and analyzed not only Pharisaic doctrines but also the ascetic preaching of the Essenes, such as that of John the Baptist.

John the Baptist's influence, evident in his call for repentance and his exemplary life, was pivotal in Jesus's decision to embrace radical change. After abandoning his prosperous business, Jesus decided to follow his mentor into the Galilean desert. This event marked a significant turning point in his life, initiating a process of spiritual transformation that was a true «rebirth».

> **By being «Born Again»**
> **you free your existence from**
> **the tyranny of reaction.**

Epiphany in the Desert

Influenced by the teachings and lifestyle of John the Baptist, Jesus of Nazareth decided to lead a more austere and radical life. He left his old life behind and ventured into the Judean Desert. This region is an arid area located east of Jerusalem, extending toward the Dead Sea and the

Jordan River Valley. In the silence and introspection of the place, he found the necessary distance to examine his existence from a new perspective.

In this isolation, he discovered the depth and scope of the concept called the «Kingdom of God», which transcended the religious and political structures of his time. Jesus had to be «born again» to understand it; he had to develop a completely new perspective. He had it clear: you can't see the «**Kingdom of God**» without this «rebirth». This refers to an **ideological reality** that goes beyond the senses and conventional reasoning. It was clear that a change in perception was imperative.

This experience is related to «**intuitive knowledge**», which manifests when a hidden truth is revealed. This does not come through reasoning or the accumulation of data. Instead, it is because the mind adjusts its focus appropriately and can see what has always been there. Jesus made it clear: «The Kingdom of God has always been among you.» It is clear that the daily reality faced by Jews, anchored as it was in traditions, rituals and privileges, made it difficult to perceive and understand the possibility of a society where the disadvantaged were blessed.

For the Pharisees and Sadducees, this premise was subversive. It threatened the order that sustained their power. You can only understand this if you have experienced a «new spiritual birth». But despite his privileged background, Jesus showed the fortitude and courage needed to go through this process. By being «reborn», he clearly glimpsed the possibility of establishing the «Kingdom of God» in Judea, with a view to expanding it to the world.

This «rebirth» of Jesus was not a matter of chance. It was the result of a rigorous and painful process in the Judean desert, accompanied by solitude, meditation, and fasting. The immersion constituted the starting point: a detailed examination of his own life, compiling experiences, ideas, and contradictions. This was followed by an overload of intuitive information that just didn't seem to be connected.

Then came the incubation stage, a period in which Jesus was tempted to return to his pleasant life. During this period of reflection and evaluation, the subconscious gradually revealed latent patterns, as if a seed were beginning to germinate autonomously in the darkness. Finally, a moment of illumination was reached. A new understanding that emerged suddenly, like a spiritual «Eureka». It was not a logical conclusion, but a revealed truth.

After this introspective journey, Jesus identified a sociology founded on divine justice and reciprocal love. This was incompatible with institutional Judaism and the injustices inherent in the prevailing power systems of the time. Consequently, he adopted an optimized view of the «Kingdom of God» that the Baptist had been preaching. This process of awakening, characterized by a rupture and reconstruction of the being, was called by Jesus «Born Again». This transformation was not merely superficial; it involved the acquisition of a new perspective, which allowed him to perceive elements that had previously gone unnoticed.

In the context of the Epiphany in the desert, Jesus clearly perceived that the most important element in social relations is the full understanding of divine love, understood as agape. This is interpreted as a theological and philosophical banquet that encompasses the totality of creation and existence. From this understanding emerged the ethical foundation of his social philosophy, characterized by a selfless, unconditional, and altruistic dedication to others, summarized in two universal ethical imperatives: «Love God above all things and your neighbor as yourself».

> *Born Again:*
> *A phrase reduced*
> *to an empty ritual,*
> *stripped of its*
> *revolutionary essence.*

Kingdom of God

The revolt of Judas the Galilean (also known as Judas of Gamala) occurred approximately between the years 10 and 13 after the birth of Jesus. This event undoubtedly marked the political climate and animosity toward Rome in Judea (Wikipedia: Judas the Galilean).

The concept of the "Kingdom of God" (Basileia tou Theou in Greek) was inherently revolutionary in the first century. In the context of the Roman Empire, the concept of a "kingdom" was exclusive to the Empire itself, and the Emperor was the only "king". The act of proclaiming a «Kingdom of God» or another "king" was regarded as sedition (*lèse-majesté*). The Roman government was concerned that such a movement could lead to popular uprisings similar to the revolt of Judas the Galilean.

> It should be clarified that the terms "Kingdom of God" and "Kingdom of Heaven" are used interchangeably. The Gospel according to Matthew uses the expression «Kingdom of Heaven», while the Gospels according to Luke, Mark, and John use «Kingdom of God». According to the most widely accepted explanation, the Gospel of Matthew is intended for Jews, who choose to avoid the direct use of God's name (Wikipedia, «Kingdom of God»).

In order to avoid serious conflicts with the Roman Empire and the members of the Sanhedrin, Jesus resorted to the use of metaphors, allegories, and parables to convey his revolutionary message. However, preaching about the meaning of the metaphor of the «Kingdom of God» admitted no concealment, since, by associating it with the messages of the Sermon on the Mount, it was understood as proposing a social order fundamentally different from that maintained by the Roman Empire and the provincial government of the Sadducees.

By advocating for a «Kingdom of God» (or «Empire of God») in an enigmatic and nonviolent way, Jesus sought to differentiate himself from armed revolutionary leaders (such as Judas the Galilean), whose inevitable fate was crucifixion and the annihilation of their followers. The employment of parables proved to be a key strategy in averting a similar outcome. The failure and violent suppression of the Judas the Galilean's revolt likely influenced Jesus's strategy.

The parable served as both a smokescreen and a sophisticated teaching method. Its radical meaning remained hidden from those seeking a purely literal, political, or military interpretation. The general public and the authorities' spies perceived the message as a simple country anecdote. This allowed Jesus to address large crowds without fear of immediate arrest for sedition.

> Jesus answered his apostles, «The knowledge of the secrets of the Kingdom of Heaven has been given to you, but not to them. Therefore, I speak to them in parables; though they see, they do not perceive; though they hear, they do not understand» (Matthew 13:11-13).

As stated in Matthew 13:11, the parable reveals its "mystery" —the deeper meaning of the Kingdom— only to those who are committed to seeking a deeper understanding: his disciples, both men and women. Specifically, Jesus used parables to ensure his closest followers fully understood his revolutionary message and to protect himself and his movement from the Roman Empire's violent repression.

However, deceiving the Sanhedrin was a more challenging task. For the Sanhedrin (particularly the Sadducees, who collaborated with Rome), Jesus's message represented a threat to the status quo. His message was revolutionary not because he promoted violence —which he always rejected— but because he referred to a form of justice that was different from the way the scribes interpreted Mosaic law. He also suggested an alternative way to access God that did not depend on the Temple or the priestly hierarchy. This alternative would have undermined the power and oppressive structures of the religious elite.

A philosophical exegesis of Jesus' central parables reveals a coherent vision of the «Kingdom of God», not as a purely spiritual concept or exclusive to the "hereafter", but as a historical, sociopolitical, and transformative reality.

- ❖ **The Mustard Seed** (Mt 13:31-32; Mk 4:30-32; Lk 13:18-19):
  This metaphor illustrates the evolutionary origin of the Kingdom. It starts out small and seemingly insignificant but eventually grows to provide universal shelter. This narrative depicts a "beginning and development over time". This organic progression is characteristic of Earth's biological and social processes. However, an eternal and immutable celestial state would not experience growth or expansion because it would be perfect and absolute from its origin.

- ❖ **Of The Yeast** (Mt 13:33; Lk 13:20-21):
  It emphasizes the internal transformation of reality. The transformative power of the Kingdom, activated by human consciousness and practice, permeates the social structure from within. The gastronomic process of dough fermenting and increasing in volume involves a chemical and temporal transformation. This process is an inherent dynamism in human history. However, the celestial is, by definition, unalterable and does not allow for the transformation that yeast represents.

- ❖ **The Sower** (Mt 13:3-23; Mk 4:3-20; Lk 8:5-15):
  Here, the Kingdom is defined as the result of "ethical and material causality". The harvest is not a metaphysical gift, but rather the result of the sower's efforts (the one who carries out the Great Commission) by placing the message of social justice on fertile ground (individuals who understand the message and act upon it). This cycle of sowing and harvesting grounds the Kingdom in human responsibility and social commitment rather than in passive inheritance in the "hereafter".

- ❖ **Of The Growing Seed** (Mk 4:26-29):
It emphasizes the "autonomy of historical social processes". After initial human intervention, social reality itself (the land) possesses an intrinsic force that generates social outcomes (the fruit) autonomously. This passage validates the historicity of the «Kingdom of God» because it emerges from the dialectic of social development. A purely celestial kingdom would lack the autonomy and stages of maturation necessary for its harvest. A celestial kingdom would be static and eternal.

- ❖ **The Barren Fig Tree** (Lk 13:6-9):
It proposes the "dialectic of radical social transformation", which is a concept that is defined by the interaction between two opposing forces, one of which is the desire for social change and the other of which is the status quo. The fig tree that bears no fruit represents social power structures that, despite having received the message, fail to produce justice for all. The warning to «cut it down» alludes to the revolution of obsolete structures. In a celestial order, "justice for all" would be an intrinsic attribute due to its eternal perfection, not an outcome subject to evaluation, crisis, or replacement.

- ❖ **Of The Hidden Treasure** (Mt 13:44):
It reveals that the Kingdom is an inherent value found in everyday life (countryside). «Selling everything» to acquire it signifies a definitive break with the current system's individualistic and oppressive ideology. This act symbolizes the being «born again» that Jesus presented to Nicodemus. This acquisition is not a renunciation in exchange for a posthumous reward but rather a total commitment to a collective project of justice, fraternity, and dignity in the present moment.

A thorough analysis of these parables and the Sermon on the Mount suggests that the «Kingdom of God» is not a heavenly realm, but rather an "earthly sociopolitical project". Rather than being a government based on domination, such as monarchy, oligarchy, or theocracy, it is a glorious social order founded on global collaboration, empowered by advanced technology, and sustained by "love of God above all things and agape love of neighbor". Therefore, although it is earthly, it is «not of this world» because is not governed by the historical principles of power and oppression of human systems.

Jesus's message maintains a "permanent critical reserve" against any system that generates spiritual or material poverty. In this sense, the **Lord's Prayer** is a liturgical tool that "politicizes faith" in the noblest way, orienting it toward caring for the community and building a just society.

From the earthly perspective we have presented and in accordance with a philosophical analysis of Jesus of Nazareth's message as a whole, the interpretation of the **Lord's Prayer** transcends the purely private, celestial realm to enter into a communal, transformative one. According to this approach, the prayer is not a plea to "ascend to Heaven", but rather an active commitment to bring "Heaven down to Earth".

- ❖ **Our Father who art in Heaven** (Mt 6:9):
  By proclaiming «our Father», the individual relationship with God is transcended. If God is the Father of all, then the logical consequence is universal fraternity. If we are all children of the Father, then no one can establish

themselves as "lord" over another. This affirmation of equality challenges oppressive hierarchies and authoritarianism directly.

- ❖ **Hallowed be thy Name, thy Kingdom come** (Mt 6:9-10): Hallow God's name involves more than ritual praise; it means acting in accordance with His will. Therefore, God's name is profaned when we tolerate misery and injustice. In this context, the «Kingdom of God» is not an otherworldly place but rather a societal project governed by the «Beatitudes». According to the Parable of the Sower, asking for the Kingdom of God to «come» means working to ensure that social structures reflect divine love and justice here, there, now, and forever.

- ❖ **Thy will be done on Earth as it is in Heaven** (Mt 6:9-10): This petition establishes the sociopolitical basis of Jesus of Nazareth's theology. «Heaven» symbolizes the fullness of justice and well-being, while «Earth» represents a reality shaped by social power structures. The prayer seeks to bridge the gap between this divine ideal and the reality of exploitation.

- ❖ **Give us this day our daily bread** (Mt 6:11): Jesus did not teach us to ask God for "my bread", but rather for «our bread». This expression reflects the idea that for bread to truly be «ours», a just distribution of resources is necessary. In a just and well-being-based society —Heaven on Earth— bread is produced to satisfy everyone's needs, so its absence constitutes a structural sin. The mention of "daily" underscores the need for daily provision, thus guaranteeing the human right to healthy, sufficient, and continuous food.

- **Forgive our debts as we also have forgiven our debtors** (Mt 6:12):
  In the original Greek text of Matthew 6:12, the word used is *opheilēmata*, which literally translates to "debts". Therefore, in a just and equitable social reality (Heaven on Earth), «our debts» refers to financial systems designed by power structures to "legally" appropriate collective wealth and perpetuate dependency. Forgiveness represents a liberation from the burdens that prevent us from living a dignified life under such structures.

- **Do not lead us into temptation** (Mt 6:13):
  This plea is not limited to personal moral temptations. It also encompasses the allure of money and our advantageous tendency to ignore social injustice instead of fighting to eradicate it.

Together, the words of the **Lord's Prayer** serve as a manifesto of resistance and a guide for Christian action in situations of exclusion. The prayer implicitly denounces unjust structures and affirms the dignity of the poor before God. The prayer provides specific guidelines for Christians living in or accompanying excluded communities, guiding them in their struggle for justice, daily sustenance, forgiveness for antisocial behavior, and liberation from the temptations caused by their economic situation.

The **Lord's Prayer** is intrinsically linked to Jesus's social philosophy and the mission he entrusted to his disciples: the Great Commission. In short, the **Lord's Prayer** is not just a pious prayer, but a "program of liberation" for situations involving the poor, the excluded, and the oppressed. (Boff, 1982; Gutiérrez, 1971; Gutiérrez, 1983).

The new social order proposed by Jesus is founded on the undisputed sovereignty of God; it is not based on human ideology or armed struggle. His radical ethic, which includes the practice of love for one's enemy, self-denial, and nonviolence, can only be achieved through a profound spiritual connection with God. While internal transformation (repentance and faith) is necessary, it is not an end in itself; rather, it represents the minimum requirement for living the radical ethic of the «Kingdom». A profound spiritual transformation, such as that described in Jesus's teachings, is fundamental to achieving positive changes in the social and economic spheres of Justice.

From the totality of Jesus' teachings, it is evident that the «Kingdom of God» is a kingdom without a king. In the Kingdoms «of this world», the King uses his supreme hierarchy to be served by others. However, in Jesus's «Kingdom», the highest-ranking individuals use their abilities to serve others, not to be served by them. Jesus did not perceive himself as a "king" of the «Kingdom of God» because he stated, «Even the Son of Man did not come to be served, but to serve» (Mark 10:45).

This approach stands in stark contrast to the Roman Empire «of this world», where Emperor Augustus declared himself «Son of God» or «Son of the Divine» to substantiate his royal authority as a God's appointed leader. It is important to note that it is erroneous to call Jesus "king," since no king has ever been distinguished for his humility nor for being a servant of humanity. In fact, not even God should be considered a "king", much less "king of kings". This is because God is far above the concept of "king". The true nature of God transcends any title or power structure conceived by humans. God's **unlimited, absolute, transcendent power** is not confined by time, space, or the physical laws that govern the earthly realm.

To define the «Kingdom of God» in its full scope, it is important to note that it encompasses all visible and invisible spheres of reality through five dimensions: substantial, natural, material, personal, and social. In its **substantial dimension**, the Kingdom represents divine sovereignty in a state of eternal perfection.

In its **natural dimension**, the «Kingdom of God» encompasses the entirety of reality, both manifested as hidden, which manifests in the universe as energy-matter. This reality comprises all known and unknown forces, governed by universal and intelligible laws inherent to it. These laws keep matter persevering in its being and advancing towards states of greater fullness and perfection.

In its **material dimension**, the «Kingdom of God» is understood as the congregation of those who have achieved «born again», who orient their life in community according to the divine principle of universal interdependence. Just as society is constituted as a group of individuals, the «Kingdom of God» is defined as a congregation of «reborn» people. Those who experience this rebirth become the "molecules" of this Kingdom, essential components that contribute to its growth and intelligible manifestation.

In its **personal dimension**, the «Kingdom of God» represents the realization of the highest human potential. This potential consists of the capacity for abstract and critical thinking, which we use to create spiritual and material realities of great social value. Experienced as a firm self-awareness, this capacity is not dependent on external sources and is sustained by a process of constant refinement.

In its **social dimension**, the «Kingdom of God» is an autonomous structure of human relations where collective wisdom comes together to maintain cohesion and advance toward higher levels of fulfillment. In this context, a coercive state is unnecessary because there is no domination of some over others, only mutual cooperation.

This social dimension finds biblical support in Mark 4:13-14 and 20 through the philosophical exegesis of the Parable of the Sower. In this passage, Jesus connects the «Kingdom of God» with tangible elements: a teacher who shares the message of the Kingdom with those who have been «born again». In the parable, the Kingdom is symbolized by seeds, the teacher by the sower, and the «born again» by fertile soil where seeds germinate and yield an abundant harvest. This harvest represents the «Kingdom of God» as the community of those who have achieved spiritual rebirth and fully comply with the Great Commission.

> *This doctrine of the Kingdom of Heaven, which was the main teaching of Jesus, is certainly one of the most revolutionary doctrines that ever stirred and changed human thought. It is no surprising that the world of that time was unable to grasp its full significance. (Wells, 1920, pp. 355-356).*

A society nuanced by «reborn people» is not a society in disorder, but order is not produced by domination.

Everyone

Jesus held that «spiritual rebirth» is a universal necessity. In order to regain the purity of childhood and «Return to God», one must free themselves from cultural bonds, beliefs, and the unwritten norms imposed by social power structures. To this end, each individual must undertake the meticulous and demanding process of being «born again». This «rebirth» fosters the development of critical thinking and access to intuitive knowledge, enabling the discovery of universal truth and the attainment of authentic freedom: that which emanates from self-awareness.

> *Jesus added*: «Do not be surprised if I tell you that everyone must be born again.»

In addressing Nicodemus with these words, Jesus urged him not only to accept the idea that everyone must be «born again», but also to recognize a transcendental truth: even he —and, by extension, the entire Sanhedrin— needed this «spiritual rebirth». Through this warning, Jesus established an irrevocable principle: no one, not even the most learned religious authorities, could enter the «Kingdom of God» without undergoing such a transformation. Therefore, the «new birth» was not an alternative, but an inescapable requirement.

Jesus trusted that a member of the Sanhedrin, someone with a deep knowledge of Scripture and Jewish tradition, would easily recognize the concept of a spiritual transformation, already present in his people's sacred texts (Ezekiel 36:25-27). Thus, the irony in Jesus's reaction when he exclaimed, «Do not be surprised if I tell you», revealed his astonishment at the incomprehension of a teacher of

Jewish law regarding a fundamental spiritual truth contained in the Torah.

> *[**Yahweh speaks to his people**]*: «*I will cleanse you from all your impurities and all your [financial] idols. I will give you a new heart and put a new spirit within you. I will remove your heart of stone and give you a heart of flesh. I will put my Spirit within you and make you to follow my statutes and carefully observe my ordinances.*» (*Ezekiel 36:25-27 [annotations added]*).

Paradoxically, it was precisely Nicodemus and his colleagues, as architects of the prevailing religious system, who contributed to creating the very structures that made this «rebirth» indispensable. Consequently, at this crucial moment in Jesus's life, his response was marked by a remarkable irony.

In this passage, Jesus carried out a systemic deconstruction of the social power structures that prevailed in the first century. In the political and social spheres of both Judea and Rome, systems of domination were characterized by the implementation of highly elaborate mechanisms of ideological and behavioral control. These mechanisms were designed to prevent the understanding of a social alternative based on social justice and conscious freedom, represented by the «Kingdom of God». According to Jesus, this "collective alienation" affected rabbis, rulers, and common people alike; no one had the ability to recognize the «Kingdom», let alone contribute to its development.

Therefore, the concept of being «Born Again» was presented as a liberating and revolutionary breakthrough, implying a «spiritual rebirth» that transcended the paradigms imposed by the Sadducees and Romans. This «rebirth» provides the freedom of self-awareness necessary to perceive reality holistically, which is defined as the ability to see the whole and its interconnected parts without focusing on one aspect. This perspective is characterized by its comprehensive and integrated approach.

That said, a clarification is in order. When Jesus tells Nicodemus that «everyone must be born again», the indefinite pronoun "everyone" refers specifically to adults who are already formed by society. Therefore, considering his teachings as a whole, we must conclude that children are excluded in this context because their innate innocence keeps them in the «Kingdom of God» until socialization removes them from that privileged status. Thus, the need for a «spiritual rebirth» applies only to adults, whose thinking and behavior have already been shaped by social power structures.

> *As it is written in Mark 10:14-15: «The kingdom of God is characterized by the purity and innocence of children. Truly, truly, I say to you, anyone who does not accept the Kingdom of God like a child will never enter it.»*

Jesus's teachings and exemplary conduct invite us to become philosophers and teachers of our own lives. This means living creatively in a continual state of communion with God.

***Constantly expand
your vocabulary
to better understand
the world around you.***

Will of the Wind

To conclude his dialogue with Nicodemus, Jesus used a powerful metaphor to highlight the fundamental effect of «spiritual rebirth» through a powerful metaphor.

> *As quoted in John 3:8, **Jesus concluded his dialogue with Nicodemus by sentencing**, «The wind blows wherever it wishes. You hear its sound, but you do not know where it comes from or where it goes. So is everyone who is born of the Spirit.»*

He expressed that those who experience this «spiritual transformation» possess a nature distinguished by autonomy and will of the wind. Here, "will" is understood as courageous assertiveness. Those «born of the Spirit» transcend rigid social structures, just as the wind is not subject to borders or controls. This new birth entails a liberated judgment, capable of discerning and promoting social systems based on human dignity and existential fulfillment. Unlike the conventional practices of social power structures, which often repress ideologies that advocate for human rights, the "renewed spirit" distinguishes itself by the questioning social injustices from a higher perspective.

Being «born of the flesh» means accepting a predetermined destiny shaped by the desires, expectations, and limitations of the hegemonic culture. Life is limited to the repetition of hegemonic patterns, without authentic autonomy or questioning. On the other hand, being «born of the Spirit» means taking on a leading and guiding role in one's own existence. Breaking away from external determination is essential in order to live with the will and autonomy of the wind: freedom of self-awareness without external constraints and with an authentic purpose and one's own direction.

Consequently, when a society is composed of «transformed individuals», it gives rise to a new paradigm: the «Kingdom of God». These reforms constitute not only change, but a radical transformation that replaces domination with social justice and oppression with brotherhood.

While traditional systems are based on hierarchies of power and unspoken privileges, the «Kingdom of God» is built on the following principles:

1. In the realm of social justice, equity is the fundamental pillar supporting equal opportunities and the protection of all individuals's rights.
2. Self-awareness is based on individual authenticity and is placed at the service of one's neighbor in particular and the common good.
3. Mutual cooperation is based on the premise of unity in diversity is raised, without any coercion.

This model seeks not merely to reform the current system, but to renew it completely. By experiencing an existence free from restrictions, except for self-imposed, each individual contributes to creating an order in which the personal and the collective are harmonized. This challenges the prevailing structures of oppression by offering a concrete alternative of fulfillment.

Jesus personified the audacity of being «born again in the spirit». With determination and conviction, he took the risk of thinking and expressing himself freely, consciously challenging the oppressive structures that Nicodemus represented. Jesus revealed to Nicodemus that his «spiritual rebirth» signaled the beginning of a new horizon: the «Kingdom of God», a reality that transcends injustice and opens the doors to a fully human world. Through the metaphor of the wind, Jesus conveyed to Nicodemus that he was no longer bound by human restrictions. He used the following allegory as a reference: «The wind blows wherever it wishes, and though you hear its sound, you do not know where it comes from or where it goes». Thus, he made it clear that his actions would be as unpredictable and free as the wind itself.

According to the Gospel of John (19:38), after Jesus's death, Joseph of Arimathea, a prominent member of the Sanhedrin, requested permission from Pilate take the body. Once he had obtained the necessary permission, he transferred the body it to a tomb. Nicodemus, another Sanhedrin member who had previously visited Jesus at night, joined Joseph. In accordance with Jewish burial tradition, they both wrapped the body in cloths soaked in fragrant ointments.

Based on this, it's clear that Joseph of Arimathea and Nicodemus could inform the Sanhedrin with certainty that **Jesus of Nazareth no longer posed a threat to their privileges regarding Roman power**. As distinguished members of the Sanhedrin, both individuals participated in the judicial body's decision to arrest Jesus of Nazareth and bring him into obedience. Thus, through just two actions, the "agent in the dark of night" fully fulfilled the mission entrusted to him by the judicial body.

> ***Jesus didn't call you to be saved, he called you to be «Born Again» and work for the «Kingdom of God».***

Synthesis

Jesus of Nazareth's fundamental philosophical concepts are presented in his dialogue with Nicodemus, recorded in chapter 3 of the Gospel of John. Jesus told Nicodemus: «Unless one is born again, one cannot see the Kingdom of God». Nicodemus expressed confusion when he asks the question: «How can a person return to his mother's womb?» Jesus clarified: «Only those who are born again through the spirit can enter the Kingdom of God. What is born of the flesh is flesh, and what is born of the spirit is spirit».

Jesus's proposal does not correspond to reincarnation or a cosmic cycle. It is neither a mythical fantasy nor a heavenly transfiguration. This transformation is a real possibility and applicable to the lives of «everyone». It is an internal spiritual metamorphosis; a radical break with the previous form of existence.

How does it happen? It is a receptive action. The individual resolutely accepts the influence of the Logos with the conviction that it will allow for personal transformation. This process involves honestly acknowledging one's own sins (state of ignorance), drawing on the faith that moves mountains», and surrendering one's will to the divine will. It is the death of the «old self» in order to achieve a new life with an authentic worldview. This metamorphosis enables us to see, understand, and take charge of our fundamental life mission: achieving the global and definitive development of the «Kingdom of God» in this life. This creates a new social life based on agape love and a new authentic autonomy aligned with divine truth.

HERMENEUTICS
ECHOES OF JESUS

Cultural Hegemony

Disconnected from its historical context, the dialogue between Jesus and Nicodemus offers a profound reflection on contemporary reality. The concepts of being «**Born Again**» and the assertive spiritual freedom of the «reborn», equated with the «will of the wind», which is invisible yet transformative and powerful, raise highly relevant questions. The correlation between the concept of the «**Kingdom of God**» and the universal demand to be «reborn» (Jesus's «everyone») requires careful consideration. First, the importance of addressing the raised question regarding the validity of the application of Jesus's call is highlighted. Similarly, the necessity of critically reflecting on the possibility of secular philosophical theories that can establish an analogy with these ideas is emphasized.

> *Hermeneutics: It is discipline that focuses on expanding the exegesis or interpretation of religious, philosophical, and literary texts. The aim is to unravel their relevance and deeper meaning in current circumstances. When approaching this discipline, it is imperative to ask questions such as: What message does this text convey in the present context? How can its original meaning be applied to the contemporary situation?*

By stating that one must be «**Born Again**», Jesus was referring not only to an individual transformation but also to collective liberation. In the context of his time, «everyone» had to be «born again» to wisely confront the dual oppression of the religious elite, primarily the

Sadducees, and the Roman Empire's political-military system, which imposed dominance through force and cultural manipulation. In this sense, the expression «**to see the Kingdom of God**» meant accepting a social alternative governed not by oppressive structures but by the harmonious and free principles inherent in nature, like those of the wind. Similarly to the way the wind acts as an autonomous force, a community that has undergone a spiritual transformation could dispense with external impositions because its members would act guided by a free and renewed conscience.

In contemporary society, freedom of conscience is achieved by overcoming the socialization processes experienced from childhood to adulthood. These processes are influenced by various institutions, such as the family, educational systems, and the media. However, the role of the family in this process is often idealized. Parents do not act as independent agents, but as products of an educational system designed by the dominant classes. Consequently, cultural patterns are transmitted to the next generation, perpetuating a chain of cultural domination.

In most countries, Ministries of Education are responsible for defining curricula, competencies, and learning objectives. Those who occupy leadership positions in these institutions are usually not selected based on proven intellectual ability, but rather on ideological affinity with groups in power. The result is a system that reproduces values and narratives that serve the established hegemony.

Implementing social education by teaching subjects such as social studies, which include disciplines such as politics, economics, and history, is an essential component of the citizenship formation process. Through these disciplines, lessons related to rights, national identity, and democratic values are transmitted from a perspective that legitimizes the established order. Although literature stimulates critical thinking, it is limited to predetermined frameworks that inhibit radical questioning.

Teachers sometimes exercise their academic freedom but operate within unclear limits. If they challenge the dominant narrative, they face a propaganda machine capable of neutralizing any dissent. In this sense, even the most brilliant minds ultimately become functional to the system unless they undergo a **critical «renaissance»**.

The healthcare sector is a particularly notable case in this regard. There is a direct relationship between the pharmaceutical industry, government representatives and directors of educational institutions. This relationship is evident in this industry's notable influence on minister and director appointments, as well as on the design of medical program curricula (Netflix, 2017). The result is a simplistic model equating health with drug use and dismissing essential factors such as lifestyle habits and preventive medicine. Medical professionals trained under this paradigm become drug promoters rather than agents of holistic health.

In this context, Jesus's words take on particular relevance, as seen in the following passage: «**Unless one is born again, one cannot see the Kingdom of God**». Neither the most illustrious scholars nor the most outstanding students can transcend the structures of domination without undergoing a radical transformation of consciousness. This requires questioning acquired knowledge, conducting independent research, and discerning which aspects of one's education deserve to be preserved and which should be discarded.

It's important to note that genuine change won't come from superficial reforms but from a spiritual and critical awakening that frees people from the invisible chains of the dominant culture. In the current context, there is a need for profound reflection on the mechanisms that allow us to envision and build a truly free society and collaborative society. This analysis marks a turning point at which we must consider generating significant changes to the social structure to achieve a new freedom paradigm that responds to the 21st-century needs and challenges.

Contemporary philosophical and sociological currents converge on the idea that culture transcends its neutral appearance to reveal itself as a sophisticated mechanism of social control. Unlike direct coercion, which is more overt, subtle manipulation subliminally modifies perceptions, values, and behaviors to preserve the status quo. This phenomenon manifests in various contexts, such as education, healthcare, art, sports, and propaganda media, establishing a deep-rooted presence in society.

Finally, we are compelled to point out that, within the framework of prevailing cultural control, marginal manifestations emerge or are permitted that, paradoxically, lend the environment an appearance of diversity and authenticity. However, these manifestations are subject to exhaustive monitoring and control. There are numerous examples of this situation, many of which have had very regrettable results.

Philosophical Parallels

Although no contemporary philosopher uses the concept of «born again» with the same socioeconomic implications as Jesus, many authors have developed theories addressing related ideas, such as radical transformation searching for authenticity, overcoming the ego, and reorienting individual and collective life. This book explores the perspectives of thinkers whose philosophical concepts resemble those of Jesus of Nazareth.

Baruch Spinoza (1632-1677)

Although they came from different contexts, **Jesus** and **Spinoza** agree that authentic personal transformation comes from a profound shift toward higher values. **Jesus**, asserts that access to the «Kingdom of God» is not achieved through external merit but through breaking with the past and focusing on unconditional love, justice, and divine truth. In his work Ethics, **Spinoza**, presents a similar process of liberation and transformation. Although he does not use the term «born again», he describes a parallel process of spiritual change that seeks happiness through the intellectual knowledge of God or nature and the control of passions.

Jesus describes those who have not experienced the «new birth» as spiritually blind and unable to see the «Kingdom of God» due to their immersion in the dominant culture. This new birth brings with it a perception that transcends previous limitations. Similarly, **Spinoza** argues that many people live in a state of «slavery» to their passions, dominated by external causes and an inadequate understanding of reality. For **Spinoza**, true freedom is achieved by transitioning from a passive to an active state where actions are guided by reason and «adequate knowledge», thereby understanding the fundamental causes of the events affecting them.

The connection between knowledge and freedom is further explored in the doctrines of both thinkers. **Jesus** affirms the importance of knowing the truth to experience significant changes in one's understanding of divine, spiritual, and social reality and to be as free as the wind. **Spinoza**, for his part, asserts that intuitive knowledge enables one to perceive the essence of things as manifestations of God, offering an immediate comprehension of everything that emanates from God's eternal and infinite attributes.

Jesus describes the «Kingdom of God» as a state of joy, peace, and full life, the fruit of a spirit transformed into harmony with God. **Spinoza** relates this to the joy derived from an increase in our power to act, known as «conatus». This term refers to an immanent universal force that keeps matter-energy persisting in its being toward states of greater perfection. In thinking beings, this manifests itself as an inherent need to acquire knowledge for survival and a fulfilling life.

Throughout his teachings, **Jesus** says that the «new birth» provides mastery of the spirit and inner peace. Similarly, **Spinoza** defines the mastery of the spirit as self-government guided by reason, freeing oneself from the passions that arise from inadequate ideas. This change signifies a transition from passivity to dynamism, aligning one with the divine.

Spinoza concludes that intuitive knowledge is the catalyst for ultimate human freedom. Intuitive knowledge frees people from their individual passions and anxieties, leading them to a state of inner peace. This spiritual and rational connection is a testament to the intellectual love for God, which is reflected in self-love and altruism toward humanity. This philosophical thought is practically identical to **Jesus's** supreme command: «love God above all things and love your neighbor as yourself».

In other words, **Spinoza's** rationalist ethics fundamentally propose an existence guided by reason and the intellectual knowledge of God. In line with **Jesus's** call to be «born again», **Spinoza** asserts that true freedom is based on liberation from enslaving passions and overcoming selfishness to achieve fulfillment.

> ***Our thought is***
> ***one of the attributes***
> ***that God shares***
> ***with the human being.***
> *Baruch Spinoza*

Immanuel Kant (1724-1804)

Both **Kant's** moral philosophy and the teachings of **Jesus** emphasize the importance of acting based on universal principles and pure intentions. This allows one to overcome selfish and utilitarian impulses in pursuit of a higher moral good.

Both **Jesus** and **Kant** agree that an internal transformation is necessary to achieve an authentic moral life that is not influenced by external factors. **Jesus** taught that being «born again» involves an intrinsic transformation of one's being and will, promoting a pure and unconditional love for God and neighbor. In this sense, he emphasizes the importance of a pure heart and genuine intention, as emphasized in the «Sermon on the Mount», which prioritizes personal attitude over mere conformity to the Mosaic Law. In other words, what really matters is not just fulfilling the external rules of the ancient Jewish Law (the Mosaic Law), but the internal motivation and attitude with which you act.

However, **Jesus** indicated that his purpose was not to abolish the Mosaic Law, but fulfill and elevate it, as evident in the following passage from his discourse: «Do not think that I have come to abolish the Law or the Prophets, I have come not to abolish them but to fulfill them». His approach transcends mere external and formal obedience, focusing on the personal attitude, motivation, and genuine intention of the individual.

The Sermon on the Mount offers a comprehensive reevaluation of moral principles, shifting the emphasis from «visible action» (compliance with the law) to «intention and disposition of the heart» (personal attitude). It is an invitation to a deeper and more rigorous morality, grounded in inner purity, love, and honesty, rather than mere obedience to external norms (Matthew 5-7).

Consistent with this, **Kant** argued that morality is rooted in the autonomous and rational will, acting out of duty rather than personal inclinations. This thesis is based on the fundamental **Kantian** ethical concept called the «categorical imperative». The «categorical imperative» is a moral mandate that regulates human conduct according to principles that can be applied universally, regardless of circumstance or space-time. It establishes that guidelines for action must be universally applicable and free from selfish motivations. Ultimately, it is an imperative moral responsibility, independent of personal or external considerations, based on intrinsic duty. Therefore, the purity of intention, rather than the results determines the validity of an action.

For **Jesus**, the commandments of the «Kingdom», such as loving, serving, and forgiving, have a universal character. This love, called «agape», is selfless and altruistic, seeking the well-being of others without expecting anything in return. Similarly, **Kant's** «categorical imperative» entails a universal moral mandate that transcends individual interests and requires acting with respect for the rational dignity of all involved.

According to **Kant**, each individual possesses intrinsic and absolute value. Using a person «merely as a means» (as a tool) constitutes a flagrant violation of their dignity. Immoral acts, such as harming a person, represent a particular problem and can have broader, more far-reaching implications. Such acts transgress a universal moral principle applicable to all rational beings. Allowing harm to occur to one person undermines the foundation of morality for all, resulting in harm at a universal level. Therefore, harm to an individual must be considered an attack on universal morality, not an isolated incident.

Jesus presents the «Kingdom of God» as an ideal that redefines human and social priorities, demanding a life guided by divine principles that transcend human laws. At the same time, **Kant** conceives of his ethics as an autonomous, rational system that elevates human beings above their sensible inclinations. He proposes a universal moral ideal.

Although **Kant** sought to develop an ethics grounded in reason, his admiration for Christian morality reveals striking similarities with the ethics of **Jesus**. Both consider selfishness an important element that must be overcome or transcended in order to achieve a higher good. This involves acting with «purity of intention» (rather than self-interest) and adopting «universal principles». Ultimately, the **Jesus's** «reborn» and the «rational being» of **Kant** strive to live in accordance with a call to act ethically, guided by will and duty.

According to **Kant's**, the rational individual possesses inherent autonomous power because reason is the only legitimate moral authority. The individual "legislates" himself through the «categorical imperative», an external law discovered by internal reason. Morality is not based on desires, tendencies, or outcomes, but on the rational imperative to act in a way that transforms our actions into universal laws. Trusting fully in his or her own reason, the individual grants himself or herself the moral law, freeing himself or herself from any external authority, whether religious or social. In this sense, moral freedom is defined as the ability to act according to a law that one has rationally created.

For **Jesus**, however, the autonomous will of the «reborn» does not emanate from human reason, but from a spiritual transformation. He illustrates the effect of «spiritual rebirth» by comparing it to the will of the wind: «The wind blows where it wishes, and you hear its sound, but you do not know where it comes from or where it goes. So it is with everyone born of the Spirit». The behavioral guidance of the «born-again» comes from a **divine inner will**. They are not influenced by imposed social conventions because their ethics are governed by «love of God and neighbor», a universal guideline that overcomes the need for external power structures because it is internal. Human behavior does not the result from rational calculation, but originates from a new spiritual nature manifested through unconditional love, or agape love.

In both philosophical approaches, morality is governed by internal principles that are immune to external influences and pressures. However, it is important to note that the origin of this principle differs in the two contexts. For **Kant**, morality is based on **reason;** for **Jesus**, it is a **spiritual transformation** expressed through agape love.

Relate to others
by recognizing humanity,
both in yourself and in others.
Immanuel Kant

Karl Marx (1818-1883)

Centuries after Jesus's death on Mount Golgotha, Karl Marx emerged as a precursor in formulating an earthly, philosophical interpretation of the «Kingdom of God». Religious institutions have historically aligned themselves with Jesus of Nazareth's sociological philosophy, but they refer to this concept as strictly theological and related only to life after death. They do not use it to refer to social, political, or, much less, material issues.

Due to this widespread historical belief, it would never have occurred to Marx to refer to the concept as a social structure based on justice and a fulfilling life. However, his materialist theory posits that revolutionary social changes will give rise to a social structure similar to Jesus's ideas of transformation and social justice, albeit without a direct or intentional connection to Jesuit theology. Thus, both Jesus and Marx concluded that the historical development of humanity would culminate in a society characterized by social justice and the full realization of human potential. Jesus called it the «Kingdom of God», and Marx called it «communism».

According to **Jesus**, human society will evolve into a socioeconomic model based on social justice and an abundant life. Furthermore, he acknowledged that this process has always existed and has been evolving since the beginning of time. «The Kingdom of God will not arrive spectacularly; it is already present among us and within us.» This gradual social transformation is driven by the spiritual development of people who have been «born again».

To this end, **Jesus** gave his disciples the «Great Commission» to spread the revolutionary social message to people of all nations. This mission will find fertile ground in individuals who accept and internalize his message. This dissemination process creates individuals who undergo a «spiritual rebirth» acquiring independence of judgment and the strength of the wind. This rebirth inspires them to sow the «mustard seed» in all nations. The result of this work will be an abundant harvest, represented by the «Kingdom of God» that will extend throughout the world. Unlike **Karl Marx**, who based his theory of economic development on materialism, **Jesus** based his theory on the power of faith, or an unshakable belief in the ability to achieve the seemingly unattainable by establishing the «Kingdom of God» throughout the world.

Similarly, **Marx** postulated that human societies would evolve into a socioeconomic system based on social justice and an abundant life. He also recognized that this process has always existed and has been developing since the dawn of history. He identified the cause of this human transformation as the material development of the «forces of production».

Unlike Jesus, **Marx** believed that the dialectical nature of the development of the «forces of production», rather than ideas, will, spirit, or faith, would constitute the determining factor of the social transformations that would lead humanity toward a socioeconomic system based on social justice and a full abundant life: «**Marxist-communism**».

However, **Marx** recognized the importance of the ideological and spiritual elements. He determined that the development of the «production forces» leads to the development of human knowledge, which consequently leads to the ideological and spiritual development of society. Once the «production forces» reach their full potential, society's high level of spiritual development enables the resumption of economic development, which had been hindered by a «mode of appropriation» that had fallen into obsolescence.

In this sense, ideological and spiritual elements are an integral part of the «production forces» responsible for the production of goods and services. This concept encompasses various material and spiritual aspects, such as scientific knowledge, technological development, the availability of natural resources, and the potential of human resources.

The concept encapsulating **Marxist theory** is known as «**historical materialism**». It focuses on the primacy of the economic and material over the ideological and spiritual as the driving force of history. Developed by **Karl Marx** and **Friedrich Engels** it is a theory that addresses fundamental aspects of society, history, and social change. In general, «historical materialism» maintains that individuals' «material conditions» and how they organize production constitute the primary factors that determine a society's structure and development. «Historical materialism» is a highly effective analytical tool for studying human history.

Within the framework of **Marxist theory**, «historical materialism» maintains that the «infrastructure» determines the social «superstructure». In this context, «infrastructure» is the purely material component of the theory, while «superstructure» represents the ideological or spiritual element.

The «infrastructure» is defined as the set of physical elements that support and facilitate the production of goods and services, thus allowing society to satisfy its needs and achieve its survival goals. The «superstructure» is the set of institutions, norms, and values that constitute the basis of social organization. These institutions encompass various aspects of collective life, including politics, the legal system, culture, education, and religion, all of which are framed by the dominant ideology.

The «relations of production» encompass the social and property relations established between individuals in the production process. These relations are determined by the «mode of appropriation» of the «means of production» (land, factories, technology, etc.) and by the distribution of the labor product.

«Historical materialism» establishes that historical economic development maintains a «**dialectical**» dynamic. Thus, economic development does not progress linearly or gradually, but rather through internal contradictions that drive society to transition from one system to another. Each economic system (or «mode of production») contains the seeds of its own destruction. New forces and tensions emerge in historical economic systems, generating imbalances that eventually lead to the disruption and the disappearance of the system as it falls into obsolescence.

In philosophy and theology, «**dialectics**» is understood as a universal force that regulates the evolution and development of all reality, whether abstract or material. When a reality reaches its maximum developmental potential, elements emerge that conflict with the original reality. Such a clash leads to the original reality»s disintegration or "death" and fosters the emergence of a new reality with a higher degree of perfection.

Just as the fundamental forces of the universe, classified as strong nuclear, weak nuclear, electromagnetic, and gravitational, are not directly perceptible through the senses, the universal force known as «dialectic» also cannot be directly observed.

According to «dialectical theory», historical social transformations arise spontaneously when the «forces of production» reach their maximum level of development. This causes the «mode of appropriation» to become obsolete and anachronistic, hindering economic and technological growth. This contradiction destabilizes the economic order, generating increasing social unrest and a chain reaction of revolutionary social changes that put an end to the current «mode of production», giving rise to a new cycle of growth. This historical process of socioeconomic development gave rise to the revolution that ended the «feudal mode of production» and gave rise to the «capitalist mode of production».

Historical propaganda has perpetuated the idea that the concept of «historical materialism» is based solely on a materialist view of human history. This perception implies a denial of divine intervention in human economic processes. Consequently, it is a theory founded on atheism.

If the aforementioned perception were correct, then it would be pertinent to analogously establish that the Parable of the Sower by **Jesus of Nazareth** also appeals to atheism. In this parable, **Jesus** proposes that the «Kingdom of God» is not established by a divine entity but develops solely through individuals capacity and actions after experiencing a «spiritual rebirth». **Jesus's** hypothesis centers on the idea that these individuals become an integral part of the «Kingdom of God» by hearing, understanding, and accepting the message. In doing so, they develop the capacity to expand its influence in the earthly world.

The key concepts of the **Parable of the Sower** are the following: the **sower** of the «Kingdom of God» message, who represents Jesus or anyone who proclaims it; the **seeds**, representing the message; and the different **types of soil**, representing individuals who receive the message. **Fertile soil** represents those individuals who have managed to be «born again», meaning those who have internalized and accepted the message, as manifested by a **fruitful harvest**. The good harvest symbolizes the spread of the «Kingdom of God» to all nations.

The only seemingly theological or religious element in this parable is the concept of the «Kingdom of God», understood as a metaphor articulating a call to action oriented toward social transformation, based on justice and the pursuit of a full and abundant life. As we have pointed out, in **Jesus's** conception, the «Kingdom of God» primarily functions as an ethical and social call to reform coexistence structures and promote equitable conditions.

If **Jesus** had intended to allude to direct divine intervention to establish and expand the «Kingdom» in this parable, the image of «fertile soil» would be superfluous given the Creator's omnipotence. The dependence on human and social conditions suggested by the «sower» indicates the necessity of a responsible human response. Therefore, the Parable of the Sower should not be interpreted as a declaration of automatic divine participation in establishing the Kingdom, but rather as a call to human action to realize it. Nor should it be interpreted as a defense of atheism. The parable's emphasis is ethical and political; social transformation requires deliberate action guided by justice and the promotion of abundant life. Similarly, we should not consider «economic materialism» to be atheistic simply because it excludes the ethical element of social action, replacing it with actions that are necessary in response to the effects of «historical dialectics». Therefore, if this parable is not based on atheism, then, by analogy, neither is «economic materialism».

If we concluded that «historical materialism» is not an atheistic theory, then we must accept that it is merely a powerful tool for historical analysis. This element of **Marxist theory** provides a theoretical framework of material and behavioral factors that allows historians to deeply and systematically understand the causes that have shaped social dynamics throughout human history.

Anti-Marxist propaganda has played a significant role in constructing historical narratives that discredit the scientific predictions of **Marxist theory**. This phenomenon has contributed to the consolidation of the idea that «communism» refers to any government that socializes the means of production and prohibits private property. Regimes that have implemented this pseudo-socialism or pseudo-communism have existed in economies that have not yet reached an advanced level of development of the «forces of production», especially technology. The system imposed under the name «**Marxism-Leninism**», developed and consolidated by Joseph Stalin in the Soviet Union during the 1920s, does not meet this essential condition.

Although Lenin implemented **Marxist ideas** in Russia in 1917, he never used the term «**Marxism-Leninism**». It was Stalin who systematized and formalized this synthesis of classical **Marxism** and **Leninism** in his struggle to consolidate his power and create an ideological orthodoxy. Evidence of this integration can be found in works such as "The Foundations of Leninism" (Stalin, 1924) and "Questions of Leninism" (Stalin, 1926). This system was imposed in a totalitarian manner and became the official ideology of the Soviet Union and numerous communist parties worldwide. However, it did not fulfill the indispensable condition of an advanced development of the «forces of production».

Marx would have called the political actors who have sought to impose **Marxism-Leninism** «utopian socialists», similar to his characterization of the English businessmen who sought to establish socialist enterprises without the necessary development of the «forces of production». **Marx** argued that these prosocial intentions were doomed to fail.

Although some countries have effective socialized health and education, the level of development of the «forces of production» necessary for the successful implementation of a comprehensive socialist system has not yet been achieved globally. Nevertheless, it is important to acknowledge that humanity is currently making significant strides in material technological development. This progress is, in turn, increasing humanity's cognitive and spiritual levels. This will lead to the dissolution of capitalism and the establishment of a genuine global socialist system. Once this economic structure is achieved, humanity will be prepared to implement «Marxist-communism» or the Jesuit ideal of the «Empire of God» on Earth. At this culmination of human development, the concepts of the «**Kingdom of God**» and «**Marxist-communism**» will converge.

In short, the «Kingdom of God» or «Marxist-communism» will emerge after technological development is accelerated by «socialism». These social structures are characterized by an absence of social classes, elimination of the state, and lack of private ownership of the so-called «means of production». Socialization these means is a fundamental pillar in the fight against labor exploitation and the unfair concentration of wealth. It promotes satisfying the needs of the entire community through productive activity. Work would no longer be alienating, fostering creativity and human freedom. Technological advances would automate most services, which would be managed by highly skilled workforce.

In both social structures, production will be organized around the satisfaction of needs, following the principle, «From each according to his abilities, to each according to his needs» (Marx, 1875). This principle establishes a foundation for social interaction based on cooperation, as opposed to competition. In this system, individuals with greater abilities would provide services to those with more pressing needs.

Religion will no longer be used by the ruling classes to control society by attributing divine meaning to people's suffering through the promise of happiness and eternal life after death. In its purest form, religion will no longer be «the sign of the oppressed creature, the heart of a heartless world, and the soul of soulless conditions» (Marx, 1844). Consequently, religion will no longer be «the opium of the people», but an ideology aimed at creating and maintaining a society oriented towards social justice and a fulfilling life.

> *Correct behavior culminates*
> *in the necessary action*
> *to change the system that generates*
> *incorrect behavior.*
> Karl Marx

Friedrich Nietzsche (1844-1900)

Once we look past the common misinterpretations of **Friedrich Nietzsche's** philosophy, a striking parallel emerges between his social philosophy and that of **Jesus of Nazareth**. This parallel is evident in the two pairs of fundamental concepts that both philosophies share: «born again» and «Übermensch», as well as «will of the wind» and «will to power».

Nietzsche advocated adopting the concept of the «Übermensch», or «superman», in order to overcome the «last man», who is characterized by weakness, conformity, and resentment. The «Übermensch» is distinguished by his ability to create his own values, affirm life, and live with a «will to power» (*Wille zur Macht* in the original German), understood as power over oneself, not over others. His critique of «herd morality» and conformity aims to foster individual greatness that transcends mediocrity and petty ambitions, thus encouraging greater commitment and excellence.

For **Nietzsche**, the «Übermensch» is a human who has transcended traditional values and «slave morality». This entails recreating one's identity, and giving new meaning to existence, thus eliminating the need for orthodox religious structures. The «Übermensch» personifies the «will to power» and sustains life on Earth, by embracing its complexity and suffering, rather than seeking solace in an imaginary paradise after death.

Despite the differences in the origins of **Nietzsche's** concept of the «Übermensch» and **Jesus's** «born again», both represent a process of radical transformation toward autonomy and affirmation of earthly life. The «Übermensch» embodies the same metamorphosis as the «born again». However, neither concept involves the irrelevant notion of an «improved man».

Nietzsche's concept of the «will to power» bears a remarkable similarity to the **Jesuit concept** of the «will of the wind». For **Nietzsche**, the concept is not simply reduced to a desire for dominion or control over others, as is often misunderstood. Instead, here we posit that this principle is much deeper and of great social value. In line with **Nietzsche's** ideas, the «will to power» is an omnipresent force permeating all existence. It emerges as a driving force that transcends Arthur Schopenhauer's mere «will to live», surpassing mere self-preservation to encompass growth, self-improvement, the expansion of one's influence, and the affirmation of life.

Every living being, from the simplest organism to the most complex human, is driven by the desire to exert power, overcome resistance, and expand influence. In the case of humans, birth ignites the spark of the «will to power» within them. This equates the will to power with Baruch Spinoza's concept of «conatus», which is ignited at the beginning of each individual's existence.

In **Jesus's** philosophy, however, the «will of the wind» is not something one acquires at birth. It is a phenomenon that results from a process of individual transformation involving sacrifice, a struggle against loneliness, and confronting social rejection. Empowerment with the «will of the wind» is the result of being «born again in the spirit». That is, in **Jesus's** case, this spiritual power is an intrinsic part of the self-awareness of the «born again» and, like the «will to power», it is power over oneself, not over others. It is an achieved virtue, not a natural condition of life.

Nietzsche proposes establishing and expanding a society similar to **Jesus's** concept of the «Kingdom of God». Implementing the social work of the «Übermensch» would require a radical reevaluation of traditional moral and ethical values. In contrast to the passive acceptance of inherited values, a critique and transformation of these values is proposed, recognizing their historical origin and their possible falsity. The goal is to establish new values based on the «will to power» and affirmation of life.

According to the presented analysis, **Jesus's** concept of being «born again» does not refer to an individual, passive «spiritual rebirth». Rather, it proposes a radical transformation of mentality that entails an active commitment to social justice. This approach requires renouncing the values inherent in an oppressive system and promoting a full and just life in the present, without delaying the pursuit of a divine reward. This process of empowerment enables individuals to experience life on Earth more authentically and fulfillingly.

In his discourse, **Jesus** refers to a «spiritual rebirth» achieved through a holistic understanding of oneself; an understanding that encompasses the totality of the person, including spiritual and social aspects. This spiritual and social knowledge entails an understanding divine truth and its relationship with humanity and nature. Thus, reflection is invited on «self-affirmation» as a method for «spiritual rebirth», as proposed by various schools of thought, such as **Nietzsche's** philosophy.

Thus, «self-affirmation» emerges as an active and creative process of forging one's destiny, living authentically, overcoming challenges, and creating values that stem from a strong and life-affirming «will to power». This approach encourages individuals to view themselves as work of art, recognizing that they are ongoing creations under their own control that are constantly evolving and developing.

Finally, **Nietzsche's** philosophy introduces the concept of «eternal recurrence» which contrasts radically with Roman Christian doctrine. It serves as a definitive test of the individual will, prompting profound reflection and prompting individuals to question whether they would be willing to replicate their current existence indefinitely. An affirmative and enthusiastic response constitutes a full affirmation of existence, disregarding the expectation of heavenly salvation or reward in the afterlife.

It is important to note that, like the prevailing interpretation of **Marx's** «historical materialism», «eternal recurrence» is often oversimplified and reduced to an atheism based solely on opposition to the dominant religious doctrine of the time. However, this opposition alone does not constitute a rational basis for atheism nor necessarily imply a rejection of **Jesus of Nazareth's** authentic social philosophy. Not believing in the dogmas of Roman Christianity (Catholicism) does not automatically equate to atheism. Neither «historical materialism» nor «eternal recurrence» are atheist theories, but rather offer fundamental interpretations or evaluations of human existence from an immanent, or "down-to-earth", perspective.

According to **Nietzsche**, Roman Christianity's social philosophy is based on what he called a «slave morality»: a value system that exalts compassion, humility, and resignation. The philosopher believed that these virtues are contrary to affirming life and the «will to power». He believed such a morality originates in the resentment of the weak toward the strong and project an imaginary reward in the afterlife. In this sense, it devalues earthly life by subordinating it to the hope of future salvation. This perspective implies a linear conception of time with a beginning and an end (the Final Judgment) and an orientation toward a heavenly reward.

This conception of transcendence sharply contrasts with the principle of «eternal recurrence», which affirms immanence. This principle compels individuals to find meaning in their present lives ("here and now") and in each of their actions, without the hope of paradise or heavenly judgment. Rather than expecting divine salvation, **Nietzsche's** hypothesis emphasizes the importance of recognizing that the meaning of life and its potential for repetition lie within each individual.

However, a thorough analysis of the concepts of «born again» and «eternal recurrence» reveals a remarkable similarity between the two philosophical frameworks. Both aim at the transformation of the individual towards a higher state of authenticity and existential autonomy. In **Nietzsche's** philosophy, individuals must transcend «herd morality» and develop their own values through the «will to power», thus achieving spiritual and creative maturity. Similarly, **Jesus's** «born again» involves a spiritual transformation that frees the individual from the shackles of legalism, both Mosaic law and Roman political domination. This transformation grants the individual a vital autonomy, which id metaphorically compared to the «will of the wind».

The result of **Nietzsche's** proposals is the «Übermensch»: the embodiment of the meaning of the earth and a model of values-creating existence, oriented toward promoting a full and abundant human life. This categorically human response emerges in the face of the collapse of religious truths and absolute values —an existential scenario depicted by the famous allegory of the «death of God». In the context of **Jesus's** teachings, the figure of the «reborn» person is emphasized. This person possesses the qualities necessary to fulfill the «Great Commission» —proclaiming the «Kingdom of God» to all nations— and is capable of revitalizing humanity toward divine justice and a fulfilling life. Thus, the «reborn» is presented as an instrument of the Spirit on Earth, and a model of an authentic, transformative existence.

In short, both **Jesus** and **Nietzsche** proposed radical approaches to achieving a full and authentic life. They both postulated the overcoming of the «old individual» (weak, dependent, and inauthentic) to give birth to a new one. In both cases, the individual acts from autonomous conviction rather than heteronomous imposition. Despite their conceptual frameworks seeming to oppose each other, they both share a profound vocation for the transformation of human beings.

> *The «Will to Power»*
> *is not a justification*
> *for political oppression,*
> *but a psychological principle*
> *of self-improvement.*
> Friedrich Nietzsche

Antonio Gramsci (1891-1937)

Gramsci's philosophy focuses on «cultural hegemony» and the struggle for social transformation. Similar to **Jesus's** concept of being «born again», which implies a disruption of established ideas, **Gramsci's** concept of «critical consciousness» entails a break with «hegemonic common sense». This phenomenon is characterized by an intellectual awakening that facilitates an understanding of social power structures and the place of individuals and collectives within those structures. This understanding is an essential step toward personal transformation.

Gramsci argued that a social revolution could not be purely economic or political, but must be preceded and accompanied by a profound intellectual and moral reform of society. This change entails the emergence of a new culture, values, and worldview on the part of the «subaltern classes».

The «subaltern classes» lack hegemonic power, which subjects them to the intellectual and moral direction of the dominant classes. This situation impedes the development of an autonomous political consciousness and a solid collective identity. The primary challenge for these groups is to overcome the prevailing hegemony and become active agents in their own historical narrative.

Gramsci emphasized the importance of «organic intellectuals», who emerge from the «subaltern classes» to contribute to the development of their class consciousness and establish a counter-hegemony. In line with **Jesus's** philosophy, these «organic intellectuals» must exhibit a mentality characterized by sacrifice and service to others. In biblical analysis, we refer to **Jesus's** statement in Mark 10:45 that his purpose in life was not to be served, but to serve and give his life as a ransom for many.

An «organic intellectual» is an individual who emerges from a fundamental social group or class to which he is intrinsically linked. The parallel between the «Great Commission» of the «born-again» and the primary function of the «organic intellectual» is striking. Their primary function is to provide their class with homogeneity and awareness of its role in the economic, political, social, and cultural spheres. These individuals, known as "brokers", primarily organize and disseminate the worldview, values, and interests that define their social class. They focus on building and preserving the hegemony of their social class, which is defined as the predominance and control of the values, ideas, and practices that guide power relations in a given society.

Gramsci's theory of «hegemony» and the role of the «organic intellectual» highlight the capacity of the «subaltern classes» to construct a new worldview and overcome the «common sense» imposed by the dominant class. While not a «divine intervention», the role of the «organic intellectual» could be interpreted as that of a catalytic agent of «collective rebirth» (**Jesus's** «everyone»). The «organic intellectual» would guide the masses in overcoming their state of intellectual and moral subordination and help them envision and eventually build a new social reality. This process involves a profound transformation, both individual and collective, with the goal of achieving an optimal state of existence. In the context of our analysis, this optimal state of existence is called the «Kingdom of God».

This comprehensive «intellectual and moral reform» can be interpreted as a «rebirth» at the social level (**Jesus's** «everyone»). It cannot be considered a mere adjustment or improvement, but rather a fundamental reconfiguration of collective identity and its guiding principles. This phenomenon entails renouncing old models of behavior and thought imposed by hegemony, giving rise to a «new form of social organization».

According to **Gramsci**, accumulating knowledge and developing theories alone are insufficient; they must be complemented by praxis or «transformative action». Social transformation requires individuals to act in accordance with their new consciousness.

This emphasis on action following new understanding aligns with the concept of «born again», which implies a new internal belief and its manifestation in a transformed life and in actions congruent with that new spiritual identity.

> **The Great Commission [Transformative Action]**: Jesus approached the apostles and entrusted them with the mission of **spreading his revolutionary theological and social message to all nations**, teaching them his principles of life and social relationships. (As quoted in verses 28:19-20 of the Gospel of Matthew.)

For «transformative action» («Great Commission») to succeed, it is crucial to break with the established order, including the kingdom of men and with «hegemonic common sense». Both **Jesus** and **Gramsci** propose the establishing a «new social order» for all human social relations. For **Jesus**, it is the «Kingdom of God»; for **Gramsci**, it is an emancipated and just society. In short, both concepts converge on the same aspiration: «Marxist-communism». However, as previously explained, the emergence of «Marxist-communism» requires more than a «new renaissance» that breaks with «hegemonic common sense». For this socioeconomic phenomenon to occur, society must have achieved optimal technological development.

The parallel between the two thinkers is striking, given their similar approaches and methods, suggesting a convergence of ideas and concepts. The concept of «born again» in **Jesus** implies an individual and collective personal transformation, affecting both individuals and communities. In line with the above, from a **Gramscian** perspective, the transformation of the «organic intellectual» emerges as a collective and sociopolitical process. In both cases, a break with a previous social state is evident in order to adopt a new and radically different one.

> *The "Ideal Society"*
> *is the result of a*
> *cultural and political struggle.*
> Antonio Gramsci

Martin Heidegger (1889-1976)

To better understand **Martin Heidegger's** philosophy, it is important to grasp the concepts of «**Dasein**», «**Das Man**», and «**finitude**». According to this perspective, «Dasein» applies to all human beings and is literally defined as «being-there», implying that each individual is thrust into life, in time and space, without their consent. By the time «Dasein» becomes aware of its existence, social power structures have already shaped its personality, including its place of birth and upbringing, language, worldview and social ideology. This process of social integration is characterized by a loss of individual identity in favor of conformity with the surrounding society. Generally, family and society mold the individual into an inauthentic person or «Das Man».

The concept of «Das Man» represents the inauthentic form of «Dasein», implying a lack of authenticity in human experience. In this sense, «Dasein», while living its life as

«Das Man», manifests itself as a singular entity that is integrated into the community, is stripped of its individuality and has adapted to the prevailing social norms without question. It is a being that was thrust into life without consent and given a personality so that it could live like everyone else. When «Dasein» becomes aware of its inauthentic existence as «Das Man», it must choose between continuing to live as an inauthentic being or becoming an authentic «Dasein», which means taking possession of its spirit develop its own critical judgment.

Another fundamental concept in **Heidegger's** philosophy is the notion of «finitude». This concept refers to a fundamental human condition being limited by time and, particular by the inevitability of death. «Finitude» is not limited to the fact that we will experience death at some point in the future, but is also a **uniquely personal possibility**. Unlike other future events, death is totally personal, non-transferable, and inescapable. This is the limit that defines our existence.

In **Heidegger's** philosophy, «inauthentic life» is characterized by an attempt to evade «finitude». We take refuge in everyday distractions, gossip, and vices to escape the anxiety produced by «finitude», or the fact that we are going to die, and become «Das Man», the «impersonal being». Authentic life, on the other hand, consciously embraces «finitude». Rather than avoiding the anxiety of death, we confront our own mortality and the limited nature of our existence. By courageously facing death, «Dasein» takes ownership of its existence and lives purposefully, recognizing that every moment is valuable precisely because of its «finitude».

For **Heidegger**, facing «finitude» leads to authenticity. When confronted with the inevitability of death, the individual is compelled to take full responsibility for their existence. This awareness of temporal limitations frees the individual from the anonymous concerns of «Das Man» and enables them to make decisions and live a purposeful life based on their own potential. The concept of «finitude» motivates the individual to reach their full potential.

In the context of **Jesus's** philosophy, the individual comes from God and remains under the divine grace of the «Kingdom of God» as a child. By the time the child becomes aware of their existence, others have already made decisions regarding every aspect of their personality and worldview without their consent. In other words, the individual is integrated into the prevailing morality of the time and excluded from the concept of the «Kingdom of God». At that moment, is faced with the choice of continuing to live as an inauthentic (ignorant or sinful) being or to be «born again» and becoming an authentic individual in a state of self-satisfaction (emancipated or saved).

The parallel between **Heidegger's** «finitude» and **Jesus's** concept of being «born again» is the radical transformation of the individual through confrontation with his own existence. Both concepts propose breaking with an inauthentic way of life to adopt a new perspective, which has repercussions on the social behavior and the conception of death.

The concepts of «finitude» and «born again» both suggest a radical transformation of the individual through an event or experience that confronts the individual with the reality of their existence. For **Heidegger**, this confrontation occurs as a result of existential angst that emerges from the awareness of one's own mortality. This anguish enables individuals to transcend an inauthentic existence characterized by the avoidance of death toward an authentic existence in which they embrace their being and freedom. Similarly, the concept of «born again» represents the beginning of a new life for the «reborn» through the power of faith. This is considered a symbolic death of the «old man» in order to adopt a new identity that lives according to the universal principles of the «Kingdom of God».

Heidegger's perspective on society focuses on the influence of «finitude» on individuals's social behavior. By adopting a stance of authenticity, a person can establish interpersonal relationships based on their unique self, freeing themselves from social pressures. This enables them to act responsibly within their community, without compromising their individuality. Similarly, the «reborn» person exhibits social conduct guided by their new moral principles, founded on service, compassion, and love. In this way, their life becomes a testament to the transformation they have undergone, and their actions are oriented toward serving others and living harmoniously in community.

Our analysis reveals a striking parallels between the philosophies of **Martin Heidegger** and **Jesus of Nazareth** concerning «finitude» or death. The core of each philosophy is how the limits of existence confer value and urgency upon authentic life. The most powerful parallel is that death is not simply the end for both philosophies, but rather the most fundamental and inevitable aspect of existence that gives purpose and meaning to authentic life.

In **Jesus's** theological and moral philosophy, an individual who achieves being «born again» no longer perceives death as an absolute end, but as a return to the divinity that made their birth possible. From this perspective, full communion with the divine dissolves the fear of death by offering the hope of «returning to God». However, those who manage to be "born again" change their perception of life and the world, and begin to live with a purpose that transcends the earthly: to fulfill the «Great Commission» of spreading the revolutionary theological and social message of **Jesus** to all nations.

Despite the expressed parallelism, the basis of each concept is radically different. On the one hand, **«finitude» is a purely secular truth**. The meaning of life and the search for authenticity arise from the awareness of nothingness and the fact that we exist in a world devoid of a predefined purpose that uplifts humanity. Liberation is achieved through the accepting this condition of being-toward-death. On the other hand, **the concept of being «born again» represents a transcendent truth**. The meaning of life does not stem from social emptiness, but from a connection to the divine. Spiritual liberation is achieved by adhering to **Jesus's** principles of social justice, which are rooted in divine will. Death represents the culmination of this connection with the divine.

> ***Thought does not consist of creating reality, but in knowing what is.***
> *Martin Heidegger*

Michel Foucault (1926-1984)

In Judea and Rome, elites maintained control over the population through physical force and ideological and behavioral control mechanisms. These systems were designed explicitly to hinder the visibility of a social alternative.

By telling Nicodemus, an influential religious and political leader, that «everyone must be born again», **Jesus** is signaling that a systemic deconstruction of the dominant structures of power in the first century is necessary. **Jesus's** conception of social justice and individual freedom, as represented by the «Kingdom of God», differed radically from contemporary perspectives. This implied an **inversion of values**, elevating the less fortunate to a position of preeminence and exalting the humblest, establishing service as the measure of greatness.

Indeed, an internal metamorphosis is imperative to adequately interpret the true components of the «Kingdom of God» and effectively contribute to its expansion. «Rebirth» was not merely a spiritual requirement, but an esencial condition for discerning and acting toward a new social and moral reality.

From **Jesus's** perspective, individuals faced not only external oppression but also internal blindness or spiritual incapacity, which prevented them from perceiving the peace and freedom the «Kingdom» offered. This limitation of vision was so significant that even Nicodemus, a prominent Judean teacher, needed a radical transformation of his perspective and being to understand and accept this new order.

In this sense, **Foucault's** philosophy is a fundamental analytical tool for understanding the mechanisms of power and control that characterize contemporary societies, particularly through his metaphor of the «**Panopticon**». The concept of the «Panopticon» is derived from the Greek prefix '**pan**' (meaning 'all'), and '**opticon**' ('seeing' or 'pertaining to sight'). The combination is, in fact, 'all-view' or 'see-all', which perfectly captures the essence of the «**Panopticon's**» total surveillance mechanism, both in its original architectural design and in **Foucault's** sociopolitical concept.

Jeremy Bentham, a utilitarian philosopher, conceived this prison architectural model toward the end of the 18th century. The purpose of the Panopticon structure is to enable the warden, protected in a central tower, to supervise the prisoners, who are located in individual cells surrounding the tower. This arrangement allows the warden to observe all prisoners in individual cells surrounding the tower without them being able to realize they are being observed (Wikipedia).

According to **Foucault**, society is a system of control in which «**normal ideologies and behaviors**» are defined to serve the interests of the dominant class. The Panopticon metaphor illustrates how power is exercised over citizens. It is crucial to note that the key lies not in actual, constant surveillance, but in this power system's capacity to maintain constant, imagined surveillance. Social institutions lead citizens to adopt the «normal ideologies and behaviors», which embody the «social panopticon». In this way, citizens become guardians of the ideologies and social behaviors. Generally speaking, citizens reject or judge the ideologies or behaviors of their fellow citizens that deviate from what has been established as «**normal**».

Social institutions, such as educational, cultural, and advertising organizations, covertly shape citizens to be acceptable to public authorities and the ruling elite. The resulting citizens, whether prisoners, workers, students, or any other members of society, feel compelled to comply with a set of rules and guidelines that regulate their behavior without the need for direct external coercion. In this sense, discipline becomes a personal, self-imposed commitment.

Consequently, contemporary society has developed a system of convert surveillance, commonly referred to as the «Panopticon», which aims to ensure that citizens conform to the established order. In this context, a dynamic of mutual surveillance and control is observed among citizens, where parents supervise their children, relatives and neighbors monitor each other, and managers and supervisors monitor their employees.

Institutions such as prisons, schools, factories, churches, and hospitals are designed to produce «docile bodies» and submissive minds that perpetuate systems of domination. The primary social objective of these institutions is to create a collective perception that solidifies specific behaviors or attitudes as «common» or «normal», and acceptable and even desirable within society. The ultimate purpose of the social structure is to align the beliefs and practices of citizens with the principles, representation, and objectives of the ruling elite without individuals perceiving this alignment as direct influence.

In his later research, **Foucault** examined the concept of «care of the self». Rather than being interpreted as a selfish act, this practice of self-reflection and introspection is presented as a set of practices (reflection, self-examination, and meditation) aimed at personal transformation. These spiritual exercises examine the relevance of personal analysis in self-realization and mastery over one's own life. This process enables the formation of authentic ethical connections with others and the world.

Through this process of self-transformation, individuals conclude that they must free themselves from societal restrictions, where «normal behavior» is determined by the interests of the ruling class rather than personal interests. **Foucault's** idea of continuous and deliberate self-transformation to achieve an optimal version of oneself is similar to **Jesus of Nazareth's** concept of being «born again».

In short, this prominent French philosopher expounded on his theory of how social power structures discipline bodies and minds, shaping individuals according to the interests of the elite. However, his work also raises the possibility of resistance and personal transformation. Through «self-care», he suggests that individuals can construct new identities («born again»), challenging imposed norms and forging subjectivities that are not limited by the system's dictates. This implies a break with the selfish, accumulating subjectivities promoted by the current order.

> *Freedom is a continuous act*
> *of fighting against*
> *the forms of power*
> *that try to define us.*
> Michel Foucault

Synthesis

We conducted a comparative study of the philosophies of seven modern and contemporary thinkers and Jesus of Nazareth. The thinkers are Baruch Spinoza, Immanuel Kant, Karl Marx, Friedrich Nietzsche, Antonio Gramsci, Martin Heidegger, and Michel Foucault. All of them, including Jesus, have made a genuine effort to give «meaning to life». Although Jesus's philosophy appears to be the most transcendental, he consistently taught how to earn the favor of the «Heavenly Father» in this life.

This comparative analysis led us to identify a transcendental yet immanent question about our existence: the «**meaning of life**». What is the meaning of life for each human being who has been thrown onto Earth without his/her consent? It is the meaning of life for all of humanity. Once we become aware of our existence and finitude, we have no choice but to give meaning to our existence.

By integrating the philosophy presented in this study, we conclude that the true «meaning of life» consist of: **taking control of our finite live and optimizing our potential, with the goal of improving the eternal life of humanity by acting as if we were humanity itself.**

This synthesis inspires us by finding a point of convergence and transcendence in the philosophies of diverse thinkers and uniting them with the central message of Jesus of Nazareth. Though each thinker approaches existence and its manifestations from different angles (metaphysical, ethical, economic, or related to power) they all strive to determine the best way to live.

The attitude consists of acting as if we are humanity itself, rejecting individualistic selfishness and embracing universal responsibility, as advocated by Kant, Nietzsche, and Jesus. The means to achieve this goal is to commit ourselves in an active and transformative way, as described by Marx, Gramsci, Heidegger and Foucault. When life has meaning, it has a direction or goal that that drives daily actions productively. Your life acquires coherence and universality (Spinoza) as it moves toward exponential development.

These philosophers have articulated an ethical principle that serves as an existential answer, giving «meaning to life» by integrating Kantian morality, Marxist social commitment, and Jesus's total self-giving.

In short, they argue that the «meaning of life» comes from a higher reality external to the individual. It is a universal vision. This is the deepest motivation that drives human beings and the organizing principle that transforms mere existence into a life with purpose, value, and meaning.

> ***The greatness of God
> resides in your being;
> discover it!***

RETURN TO GOD

The Concept

The concept of «Return to God» accurately summarizes Jesus's preaching about our permanent and eternal relationship with God, which exists before birth, lasts throughout life, and extends beyond death.

This concept identifies the most significant moments in our relationship with God, such as childhood, adulthood, and death. The concept of «Return to God» is a meticulously structured vision that highlights specific life moments in order to define human relationships with oneself and with others in the context of the divine relationship.

- ❖ During **childhood**, the connection with the «Kingdom of God» is an inherent, a natural state.

- ❖ During **adulthood**, although God never abandons us and remains within us, our conscious connection with Him weakens. Restoring it requires a voluntary and radical act of transformation: being «Born Again».

- ❖ At **death**, the «Return to God» is an inevitable and universal event, occurring when the journey of life has concluded.

The concept of the «**Return to God**» as an event that occurs only at two specific moments in adulthood —when one is «**Born Again**» and at death— provides a philosophical framework for Jesus of Nazareth's concept of salvation or emancipation. In this context, transformation during life is not merely an option, but the only path to reestablishing one's relationship with the divine before death.

Despite being a novel synthesis of his teachings, the concept of the «Return to God» can be considered an integral and coherent part of Jesus of Nazareth's theological philosophy. It does not introduce a foreign idea, but rather organizes three elements scattered throughout Jesus's preaching in a logical and existential manner.

- **The purity of a child, a fundamental attribute of the «Kingdom of God»**: Jesus himself established the principle that children are intrinsically linked to the «Kingdom of God» and affirmed that to access said «Kingdom» one must aspire to the purity of a child. The concept of the «Return to God» legitimizes this initial connection. This premise aligns perfectly with Jesus's statement in Luke 18:16-17: «The kingdom of God belongs to those who are like children. Truly, truly, I say to you, whoever does not accept the kingdom of God like a child will never enter it».

- **«Born again», is an indispensable condition for the «Return to God» in life**: The heart of the concept of the «Return to God» lies in the redefinition of adulthood. According to our analysis, an adult is someone who has consciously lost their connection to the «Kingdom of God», and the only way to regain it is through a voluntary act of transformation: being «Born Again». This premise aligns perfectly with the dialogue between Jesus and Nicodemus, recorded in the Gospel of John.

- **Death is the ultimate «Return to God»**: The idea of that death is the final stage of the «Return to God» is a central theme in Jesus's eschatology. This return ensures that, no matter one's life path, the final destination is fulfillment in the divine presence.

Socio-Theological Criticism

Those in positions of social and financial power structures manipulate religious and moral concepts to obtain personal benefits. Political and religious institutions, for example, create a socioeconomic system in which problems and failures are attributed to individuals, while the true systemic causes remain hidden or are even promoted by these elites.

The concept of original sin and the need to confess sins, embodied in the phrase «mea maxima culpa», is established as a mechanism for internalizing the cause of sins or ignorance. By making each individual perceive themselves as imperfect and responsible for their mistakes, attention is diverted from the sociopolitical system's shortcomings. Promoting this worldview of sin or ignorance directs people's attention toward personal redemption rather than questioning the social, economic, and political conditions that generate inequality, crime, and violence.

These conditions, consequently, shape the social and even personal behavior of ordinary people. Social power structures implement a culture of individual guilt or ignorance to position themselves as judges and executioners. This gives them the power to incriminate and sentence individuals as «responsible» for social problems, such as crime, vagrancy, theft, aggression against others, and hatred based on origin. This imposed culture justifies the implementation of punishment systems, such as prisons, as a necessary response to personal «sin or ignorance».

In this cultural context, poverty and social inequality are tolerated because they are considered part of an inevitable human reality, where individuals are responsible for their socioeconomic conditions. Social power structures benefit from the existence of these problems and, furthermore, present themselves as the only solution and benefactors by implementing social welfare systems.

The «Kingdom of God» in childhood is not a conscious choice of the child but an inherent condition of their nature. Children are an intrinsic part of this «kingdom» because their existence is not contaminated by social power structures. This state of purity, in which the child is naturally connected to the «Kingdom of God» is interrupted by social power structures without the child's consent.

In this context, ignorant or sinful adulthood is not the result of a purely free choice, but rather the outcome of developmental processes and socioeconomic conditions designed and maintained by social power structures that disrupted the original connection with God. These processes and conditions imply alienation, a situation outside the will of individuals in which they are not considered ends in themselves, but rather a means or mere tools for social power structures to serve and benefit from.

This social reality contradicts the principles Jesus taught. In Matthew 20:28, he said, «I did not come to be served, but to serve». In reality, social power structures appear to serve the citizenry when, in essence, they are served by it. Therefore, the «fall of man» was not caused by his disobedience nor by the guilt or ignorance of the woman, but by the corruption of social power structures that raise some children to be docile servants while abandoning the majority to their fate. These social processes draw children away from the «Kingdom of God», creating the need to be «born again» to «Return to God».

This approach offers a unique interpretation of the concept of «Return to God», distinguishing it from traditional ideas of divine judgment, punishment, or reward. According to our thesis, which is based on a profound social critique, hell is a metaphor for the social injustice perpetrated by power structures, not a place of eternal divine punishment for ignorant or sinful individuals.

According to this interpretation, hell is not a demonic realm, but rather a state of social injustice. Power structures, represented by the devil, are what create conditions of inequality that push individuals to commit antisocial acts. These same structures then act as judges, punishing those who have engaged in criminal or immoral conduct. In this allegory, the «eternal fire» represents the torment of this perpetual oppression.

According to this view, the «Return to God» is not about final judgment, but about liberation from this cycle of systemic oppression. Both in the spiritual life and after death, the individual is detached from earthly power structures and injustices. Our thesis suggests that God is the eternal refuge for all of his creatures and not a demon who punishes individuals for actions that are the logical result of social injustice and the alienation of people.

Essentially, our thesis termed «Return to God» separates divinity from the primitive concept of earthly punitive justice. It attributes guilt or ignorance for human actions to social power structures rather than to the morality created and divinized by those structures.

Praxis

Based on the social justice concepts of Jesus of Nazareth, this analysis calls for a critical reflection on the origins of social problems and how social power structures use morality to perpetuate systems that benefit them. In this context, it is necessary to logically apply Jesus of Nazareth's thesis, which asserts that «everyone» must be «born again» to liberate themselves from the «herd mentality» and understand the true causes of sin or ignorance. This knowledge empowers you to understand the world and yourself. It breaks the chains of sin, ignorance, prejudice, and limitations. It grants you autonomy and the capacity for self-determination. The «reborn» person who acts in this way has undoubtedly achieved the «Return to God».

Church members are often perceived as individuals who display a devout commitment to their faith by strictly adhering to the religious teachings and practices established by their ecclesiastical institution. However, their devotion does not necessarily align with the concepts of being «born again» or the «Great Commission», two principles considered essential to being part of the «Kingdom of God» in the theology of Jesus of Nazareth.

The concept of «born again», originating in the New Testament specifically in the Gospel of John, refers to a profound and personal spiritual transformation. It is not merely a modification of behavior or observance of religious precepts, but an inner transformation achieved by completely believing that we must take charge of our lives and act accordingly. A person who is «born again» experiences a fundamental change in their relationship with the divine that transcends mere adherence to the practices of a religious institution.

While church members demonstrate great love and devotion, the primary focus of their faith often remains within ecclesiastical structures. Their faith may be very personal and sincere, but if it is not translated into action, or praxis, of the «Great Commission», it could be perceived as incomplete from Jesus's theological perspective. This inaction, restricting faith to prayer and praise without active involvement in the world, could explain why, despite their devotion, they have not been «born again» or part of the «Kingdom of God» in this life.

The so-called «Great Commission», as recorded in the Gospel of Matthew, is a mandate given by Jesus to his followers to spread the gospel to all nations. This call is addressed not only to clergy and ministers, but to all believers. Therefore, it is imperative that Christians promote their faith beyond the walls of the church in other areas of the social and political order.

This perspective suggests that faith must be both interior («Born Again») and exterior («Great Commission») to be complete and meaningful. It's important to note that religious devotion isn't limited to personal or church setting, it also encompasses actions in the global context.

The «Great Commission», as established in the Gospel of Matthew, urges believers to spread the message and faith to all nations. Traditionally, this commission has been interpreted as a task of personal evangelization, understood as disseminating the message of faith exclusively to individuals. However, an interpretation based on the entirety of Jesus of Nazareth's teachings implies that faith includes a component of social transformation. From this perspective, a faith-based mission seeks not only to transform people's hearts, but also to reform the social power structures that perpetuate injustice, sin, and ignorance.

These structures, including governments, corporations, and financial institutions, have a significant influence on individuals's lives. Often driven by the pursuit of control, wealth, or influence, these social structures can, intentionally or unintentionally, create systems that are unfavorable to the most vulnerable. Therefore, sharing Jesus's teachings with these structures is not just proselytizing; it is ensuring these institutions operate under the principles of justice, equity, and community service.

The fundamental premise underlying the need for the «Great Commission» to focus on of social power structures is the conviction that transforming these structures can generate large-scale social impact. Rather than addressing only the symptoms of injustice at the individual level, such as poverty or exploitation, this strategy identifies and addresses the underlying causes of these problems.

Intervening in the policies, laws, and values of these powerful institutions could achieve a deeper, more lasting transformation. For instance, rather than providing ad hoc assistance to homeless individuals, we should advocate for comprehensive reforms to public education, employment, and banking policies and practices that hinder access to decent housing or lead to housing loss. This approach does not replace individual evangelism but complements it by arguing that authentic faith must be manifested in personal life and in the pursuit of systemic justice. According to this perspective, the synergy between individual conversion and structural transformation gives faith a universal vision, or the «power to move mountains».

In short, linking the concepts of «Born Again» and the «Great Commission» with their application in social power structures offers a perspective that transcends traditional interpretations. This analysis enriches theology and anchors it in the reality of the world, where social power structures directly influence individuals's lives.

Reflecting on how faith can impact large-scale decision-makers, it can inspire individuals, especially religious ones, to perceive their spirituality as a force for social transformation toward full justice, not merely as a path to personal salvation or emancipation. This vision urges people to transcend individual devotion and seek a faith that manifests itself in justice, equity, and service to others, especially those who have not been «born again» in a social or economic sense.

Therefore, the «Return to God» after death is a logical conclusion that completes the cycle of human existence. Death is the only guarantee that all individuals will ultimately achieve the «Return to God», regardless of whether they were «Born Again» in life. It's important to note that the «Return to God» at death is not a reward for a moral life, but rather an act of universal grace. This process involves restoring the original connection established during childhood. It is an inherent part of the laws of the universe established by the Creator, such as the laws of universal gravitation, conservation of energy, and thermodynamics.

Consequently, the concept of the «Return to God» is related to the philosophy of Jesus. It is a philosophical interpretation of Jesus's teachings, that organizes and gives new coherence to concepts traditionally interpreted atomized or disjointedly. This concept provides a temporal and existential framework for the individual's journey, from birth to death, within the «Kingdom of God».

Thus, our thesis on the concept of «Return to God» has the potential to be a powerful tool for dialogue about how faith and social action can come together to create a more just world-fulfilling the mandate of the Parable of the Sower.

«The Truth will set you free», "freeing us from manipulation and conformity.

A Philosopher Called Jesus
(7 BCE-27 CE)

His Philosophy

Our biographical analysis of Jesus of Nazareth has focused on his earthly legacy, recognizing him as an exceptional human being and an outstanding thinker. This work addresses an essential part of Jesus of Nazareth's philosophy: the Jewish man born in 7 BCE who grew up, lived, experienced a «new spiritual birth», and died in Judea in 27 CE at the age of thirty-three.

Jesus's philosophy centers on the concept of the «Kingdom of God». Predominant Christian traditions interpret this «kingdom» eschatologically, as a latent reality that will be fully realized with the Second Coming of Jesus Christ. At that time, the Earth becomes the «Kingdom of God», ruled by Jesus Christ, God's only begotten son, and «King of kings».

It's important to note that the concept of the «Kingdom of God» existed before Jesus. John the Baptist announced its imminent arrival. However, Jesus of Nazareth gave the concept a profoundly social and earthly meaning. Through the Parable of the Sower, Jesus entrusted the task of working for this «kingdom» to those who are «born again», meaning those who renew their understanding, listen to and comprehend his message. It is these individuals who, through continuous commitment and effort, will ensure the «Kingdom of God» is fully manifested in earthly life.

The call to be «Born Again» is a profound invitation to inner transformation that implies a change in values and priorities. The «Kingdom of God» is not merely a vision for the future, but a way of life in the present, founded on agape love, justice, compassion, and selfless service. These virtues opposed selfishness, excessive competitiveness, and accumulating wealth as the primary objective. From this perspective, personal «rebirth» is an essential requirement for social transformation.

Jesus's proposal transcends the religious realm and takes the form of an ethical and social call. The concept of the «Kingdom of God» is not merely a promise of a passive afterlife, but a transformative project that must be built by those who have experienced a «spiritual rebirth». This «rebirth» implies a profound transformation, both individually and collectively, advocating for justice, compassion, and equity in the world.

Revolutionary Content

Jesus's philosophy is characterized by his firm opposition to indifference toward the suffering of others. According to him, a just society ensures equal opportunities and proclaims empathy as its guiding principle. «Born again» people, driven by altruism and compassion, adopt a leadership approach characterized by humility and a vocation for service. They listen attentively to the demands of the oppressed and respond with patience and solidarity, rather than imposing their authority.

Jesus's leadership model contrasts sharply with the oppressive systems of his time and ours. The so-called «heirs of the Earth» are not those who resort to violence or ambition, but rather those who demonstrate meekness and lead without exercising dominance. Jesus taught that leaders should serve the people, not be served by them. Those who are «born again» do not pursue the accumulation of wealth or influence. Rather their primary goal is to satisfy the «hunger and thirst for righteousness», ensuring an equitable distribution of opportunities and resources.

In the context of the «Kingdom», justice is oriented toward restoration rather than revenge. Jesus criticized legal systems that punish without offering rehabilitation and social structures that exclude those who think or act differently (Luke 23:43). According to his philosophy, true justice is based on active compassion, manifested through the rehabilitation of ignorant or sinners, forgiveness of debts, welcoming of strangers, and prioritization of the common good over individual interests.

Jesus's philosophy is not based on a contemplative utopia, but rather constitutes a call to action to build a society in which the last come first. The Parable of the Sower illustrates that the «Kingdom of God» is not achieved through isolated miracles, but through the ongoing efforts of those who have experienced a «spiritual rebirth» and strive to build a society founded on justice, empathy, and mercy. In this sense, his message is profoundly revolutionary, challenging indifference and promoting changes in everyday life.

Jesus of Nazareth formulated his proposal in an oppressive context, in which political and religious authorities collaborated to maintain a status quo of indiscriminate oppression and domination. His vision of the «Kingdom» had spiritual and political implications, offering a radical critique of Roman imperialism, Sadducee collaboration, and Pharisee legalism. Understanding this context is essential to comprehend why his philosophy was perceived as subversive and why he was treated as a political threat.

Some of Jesus's teachings that have been deliberately ignored by religious orthodoxy due to their revolutionary nature and their potential to challenge social power structures. Notable examples include his critique of wealth and the idea that it is difficult for the rich to enter the «kingdom»; his rejection of violence, exemplified by turning the other cheek and loving one's enemy; and his exaltation of service and selflessness, as seen in the idea that the first will be last and the servant of all. These postulates directly threaten structures sustained by force, accumulation, and ambition.

Distortion of his Message

The transformations promoted by the Roman Catholic Church around the figure of Jesus have certainly led to a significant dissociation between its philosophy and human social life. The Roman Jesus is not recognized as the Messiah awaited by the Jews of Judea, nor as the prophet, teacher, or rabbi who preached among his people. Rather he is conceived as one of the three manifestations of God.

This reconfiguration involved a transition from being a Jewish philosopher in Judea to being a divine incarnation. This shift elevated his teachings to a transcendent level, practically relegating them beyond earthly life. Jesus's role as a teacher and role model underwent a metamorphosis, turning him into an object of worship and an abstract theological construct with complex practical applications. At worst, he became nothing more than an ornament for clothing. At best, he became a symbol of religious institutional status.

After his death, this cultural distortion was exacerbated by the appropriation and reinterpretation of his teachings by Paul of Tarsus and, later, by the Roman Catholic Church. These processes primarily served political ends. Paul directed his preaching toward the Gentiles to expand the community of Jewish believers. Meanwhile, Roman political leaders took advantage of the growth of Pauline Christianity to create a deity that would help them restore the Empire's cohesion and consolidate their power. Consequently, many of the socioeconomic and revolutionary elements present in the original preaching were attenuated or displaced toward doctrines centered on individual salvation. Nevertheless, we must recognize that without Paul of Tarsus' legacy, we probably would not know Jesus of Nazareth today

Despite becoming a «Born Again» as a social figure, Jesus of Nazareth was unable to completely separate himself from his cultural and religious context. Consequently, his ideas were undoubtedly influenced by the customs and Mosaic law of Judaism. Therefore, his social philosophy retains a marked theological tone. The ethic of the «Kingdom of God» and loving one's neighbor as a manifestation of love for God and accountability to God are central components that influenced his conception of life in society

Jesus's most emblematic teachings are recorded in chapters 5 through 7 of the Gospel of Matthew, also known as the Sermon on the Mount or the Beatitudes. These passages denounce social injustices in Jesus's environment. In the Roman Christian tradition, these passages are often presented as a guide to personal piety, emphasizing humility and mercy. However, this tradition was conceived to foster conservative communal morality, also known as «herd morality», which deactivates the transformative potential of these teachings.

When analyzing the passage in which Jesus states, «Blessed are those who suffer and are hungry, for they will be comforted», one can infer that the original meaning lies in the promise of an alternative social order —a «Kingdom» without hunger or oppression— and not necessarily in a call to passively accept suffering in this life.

Consequently, Jesus's philosophy poses a genuine challenge to established social power structures. However, religious institutions tend to neutralize or dilute innovative ideas when integrating them into systems established by ruling classes. By incorporating theological and symbolic elements that encourage inaction during one's lifetime, these institutions have rendered Jesus's ideas less applicable to earthly sociopolitical systems, ranging from the Roman Empire up to the current power structures. It is also important to note that contemporary mainstream theology rarely addresses certain aspects of his teachings due to their incompatibility with prevailing doctrines.

These cultural and political dynamics have limited and distorted Jesus's social and revolutionary philosophy.

Consequently, he has not been recognized as one of history's great philosophers, on par with Socrates, Plato, Aristotle, Descartes, or Kant, who also addressed social, ethical, and political issues of universal scope.

It is imperative to overcome the barriers erected by social power structures. Just as happened with Nicodemus, the established powers are not interested in Jesus's radical ethics because applying them would mean losing their power and social privileges. These structures have been designed to elevate Jesus to deity status, ensuring that his philosophy cannot be applied to earthly sociopolitical systems such as the Roman Empire, capitalism, and the Vatican's wealth, among others. Furthermore, many contemporary theologians do not adequately address the philosophical concepts of Jesus because they are incompatible with current theology curricula. This institutional theology hinders the authentic application of Jesus's philosophy to earthly sociology.

One of the main objectives of this work is to update institutional theology by applying the earthly sociology of Jesus. Presenting Jesus as a philosopher poses methodological challenges. Initially, his teachings were transmitted orally. Subsequently, they were transcribed in various contexts, introducing variations and divergent emphases in the Gospels. Additionally, reinterpretations and institutional priorities have, over the centuries, privileged doctrines of ritual and social control (salvation, sacraments, and a monarchical ecclesiastical hierarchy) over the more radical elements of Jesus's preaching.

Synopsis

A thorough examination of texts such as the Sermon on the Mount, the metaphor of the «eye of the needle», the Parable of the Great Banquet, the dialogue with Nicodemus, the Parable of the Sower, and the «Great Commission» reveals a philosophical proposal with evident social and political implications. These passages articulate principles for a radically different social order, including reversing hierarchies, equitably distributing goods, ensuring justice for the marginalized, and practicing unconditional compassion. Together, these principles comprise a philosophy of revolutionary social order. The scope of this philosophy demands recovery and reexamination from historical, theological, and sociological perspectives.

Stripping Jesus's teachings of dogmatic and religious restrictions and examining them from a philosophical perspective, reveals a fundamental conclusion: his discourse constitutes a philosophical system of radical change and comprehensive transformation, both at the individual and collective levels.

This philosophical analysis shows that the traditional religious interpretation of the concept of «born again» as a mere dogmatic adherence to the cult of Jesus Christ, is an inadequate understanding of the concept. It lacks relevance to practical life. This inadequate perspective not only contradicts the teachings of Jesus of Nazareth, but also specifically opposes his Parable of the Sower, which emphasizes ethical transformation and human responsibility throughout world history.

> *The Spirit of the Lord is upon me,*
> *to bring good news to the poor*
> *and to set free*
> *those who are oppressed.*
> — *Jesus of Nazareth*

POEM
EPIPHANY IN THE DESERT

The Jordan wind blew gently, soft and slow,
caressing the desert with a sweet glow.
It carried teachings, filled with awe and might,
voices that broke the routine with fervent light.

Jesus, the son of a world of stone and wood,
heard the silent calling where he quietly stood.
Fully alone, he shed his angles and fine forms,
and went into the desert, escaping life's storms.

Among the dunes like pages waiting to be read,
He deciphered the dust and the life that it fed.
The kingdom wasn't a place with borders or walls,
but an open eye and a vision that calls.

An eternal fire burning without trace,
«Be born again, Jesus», it whispered with grace,
while he learned, with his eyelids tightly closed,
to see an infinity of dreams disposed.

It was a birth in reverse, reborn to the core,
where the soul is a seed, waiting to soar.
Reason, the carpenter's only simple tool,
was forgotten in a cold and severe pool.

And wonder sprouted in his divine being,
a Eureka! that brings a bright and shining seeing,
a light that logic can never truly reach,
breaking the chains, allowing him to preach.

POEM EPIPHANY IN THE DESERT — BORN AGAIN

The Kingdom's truth has always been so near,
its seeds are scattered widely, sharp and clear.
But the sightless led by custom and fear,
do not put down deep roots to grow right here.

Sadducees and Pharisees, in their ritual maze,
felt their foundations tremble in a fearful haze,
before this truth that unmasks the long-kept scrolls,
with mighty shouts that echo in their very souls.

Only the reborn, who have drunk the silent cup,
down to the last bitter and lonely drop,
now see the Kingdom of God: a world of eternity,
though by many scorned for its great verity.

Jesus declared: «Here I am, dressed in light,
sharing the love I have possessed with all my might.
Let us all be reborn in this clarity!
Thank you, Father, for dressing me in verity!»

«Here I stand, in my renewed state,
the child who was reborn by fate.
Even though my life they will end,
Those who refuse to truly ascend.»

PARABLE
A TRUNCATE ENTERPRISE

Three days after Jesus was crucified, two of his many disciples set out on the road for Emmaus, a village located eleven kilometers from Jerusalem. As they walked, they talked about the recent events that had occurred, feeling sorrowful. During their conversation, a man approached them and joined their journey. The man calmly asked them a question:

«Excuse me, what are you talking about so intensely?»

The disciples stopped and looked sad. Cleopas, one of the disciples, responded with a question of this own: «Are you perhaps the only pilgrim in Jerusalem who is unaware of the events of the last few days?»

«Could you specify what events concern you?» The man inquired.

«I am referring to what happened to Jesus of Nazareth», Cleopas explained. «He was a prophet who performed great works and spoke with great authority before God and the people. The chief priests and members of the Sanhedrin handed him over to the Roman authorities, who condemned him to death and crucified him. We expected Jesus to be the liberator of Judea. However, three days later, some women in our group surprised us. They went to the tomb at dawn but did not find his body. They reportedly declared that they had witnessed an angelic apparition that had communicated the news of his resurrection. Upon learning this, some of us went to the tomb and confirmed that it was empty.»

Parable A Truncate Enterprise — Born Again

As they continued on their way, other travelers joined them, drawn by the conversation, as if by an invisible force were calling them to share this story. Soon, a large group joined them.

At that moment, the man said to them, raising his voice: «How lacking in understanding you are, and how slow to grasp the message of your liberator! Didn't your liberator entrust you with a mission for all of Judea and the ends of the earth? What are you waiting for? A great puppeteer? If so, then surely **all of you need to be born again**.»

Everyone stopped and surrounded him with astonished gazes. After a moment of silence, during which an air of anticipation was palpable, the man began to tell them a parable.

«Once upon a time, there was an enterprise dedicated to the restoration and construction, of various buildings, such as homes, bridges, temples, and schools, in stone and wood. Its leader, a wise and experienced man, gathered his workers every Sunday to remind them of the purpose of their work: to heal what was broken, strengthen what was weak, and build what was needed.

»His words resonated like a light, inspiring in them a deep desire to serve. He spoke to them about the importance of unity and a shared vision, and of the pride that comes from being part of something greater. He provided them with a clear and precise vision, and they were leaving these meetings with renewed fervor, sharing the leader's message, as if they were people who had just attended a symphony concert.

»Furthermore, the leader used to organize workshops in which all the workers were reflecting on the team's challenges and strengths together. These Sunday meetings were held weekly throughout the years, and were planned with great care. However, despite calling themselves "builders" and referring to the enterprise's mission as the "Great Commission", the workers never left the workshop to carry out any restoration or construction.

»The facility had a wide range of precision tools and its workers possessed a vast array of construction knowledge. Nevertheless, the cracks in the city continued to spread, and the demand for housing and buildings continued to rise. The community needed this enterprise's services, which never materialized. While this enterprise was impeccable in theory, it lacked tangible results in practice. It's about a Truncate Enterprise.»

> ***What you failed to do***
> ***for the underprivileged,***
> ***you did not do for Me either.***
> *God*

EPILOGUE

I found this book fascinating to read! I feel imbued with great hope! It certainly offers an extraordinarily powerful and highly inspiring perspective. Despite their different philosophical frameworks, figures as diverse as Jesus of Nazareth and thinkers from different eras agree that human and their political and religious institutions have the capacity to create a world based on loving one's neighbor and ensuring justice for all. They simply need to dare to break with the hegemonic culture.

The Hope for a Reborn World: If this interpretation of Jesus's philosophies and those of other prominent thinkers is correct, then the human capacity to transcend selfishness, ruthless competition, and the obsession with the «exploitation of man by man» is not a chimera, but a possibility inherent in our being.

This implies that we are not fatally condemned to a world dominated by extreme savage capitalism. If we can be «born again» as individuals and as a society, recognizing our universal interconnectedness (Spinoza), acting according to ethical principles (Kant), freeing ourselves from alienation (Marx), overcoming mediocrity (Nietzsche), forging a new hegemony (Gramsci), living in society with individual authenticity (Heidegger), and remaining aware of the dangers of normalization (Foucault), then a world founded on love, peace, freedom, and egalitarian economic prosperity will be within our reach. This vision is not an unattainable utopia, but rather a project for which humanity possesses the necessary spiritual and intellectual tools.

Therefore, the transcendental task of the «born again» in humanity is **praxis**: translating this understanding and hope into actions that shape our societies toward these ideals.

We must stop thinking that the government or God must act for us. We must understand that we must be «born again» to acquire the «will of the wind» to act on our own.

What concrete actions do could you take to improve the world, society, your family, and your relationship with your partner once you are «**Born Again**»?

With fraternal hope,
Jose A. Alegria-Morales
Archipelago of Enchantment,
Puerto Rico

A soul transformed by
Born Again
aims for truth
and unmasks deception.

REFERENCES

All biblical references are taken from the Christian Standard Bible (CSB), published in 2017. Holman Bible Publishers. BibleGateway.com.

The parable "A Truncate Enterprise" included in the eponymous chapter of this work is our own creation. However, the narrative of the disciples walking towards Emmaus and their initial conversation with the man who joined them on the road comes from the biblical passage in the Gospel of Luke, chapter 24, verses 13-26.

Alegria-Morales, J.A. (2023). Abba's Kingdom: The Kingdom of Truth (AMZ Publishing Pros) (Amazon ebook & Paperback - Apple Books ebook)

Alegria-Morales, J.A. (2025). FINALLY! The Manifest Truth: Chronicle on Israel and Palestine. (Amazon ebook & Paperback - Apple Books ebook).

Boff, L. (1982). Lord's Prayer of Integral Liberation. (Amazon Kindle & Paperback).

Díaz Genis, A. (2010). The eternal return of the same in Heidegger's Nietzsche. Estudios Nietzsche, (10), 67-82. https://doi.org/10.24310/EstudiosNIETen.vi10.10183.

Fernández Liria, C., & Alegre Zahonero, L. (2018). Marx from zero: For the world to come. Universidad Complutense.

Fernández, O. (2011). Mariátegui and Marxism. In C. Drago, T. Moulian, & P. Vidal (Eds.), Marx in the 21st century: The validity of (the) Marxisms (s) for understanding and overcoming current capitalism (pp. 197-210). LOM Ediciones.

Foucault, M. (2008). Discipline and punish: The birth of the prison (A. Garzón del Camino, Trans.). Siglo XXI Editores. (Original work published 1975).

García Ninet, A. (1971). The problem of eternal recurrence in F. Nietzsche. Estudios Filosóficos, 20(55), 555-568.

Gramsci, A. (1981). Prison notebooks (V. Gerratana, Ed.; A. Granados & M. H. de Granados, Trans.; Vols. 1-6). Ediciones Era. (Original work written 1929-1935).

Gramsci, A. (1984). Historical materialism and the philosophy of Benedetto Croce (J. Aricó, Trans.). Ediciones Era. (Original work written 1929-1935).

Gutiérrez, G. (1973). A Theology of Liberation: History, Politics, and Salvation. Translated by Sister Caridad Inda and John Eagleson. Maryknoll, New York: Orbis Books. First published: Teología de la liberación: Perspectivas, 1971.

Gutierrez, G. (1983). We Drink from Our Own Wells: The Spiritual Journey of a People (Amazon Kindle & Paperback). First published: Teología de la liberación: Perspectivas, 1971 (English translation, 1973)

Heidegger, M. (2007). Being and Time (J. E. Rivera, Trans.). Editorial Universitaria. (Original work published 1927).

Kant, I. (2009). Critique of Pure Reason (M. Caimi, Trans.). Fondo de Cultura Económica. (Original work published 1781/1787).

Kant, I. (1785). Groundwork of the Metaphysics of Morals (Grundlegung zur Metaphysik der Sitten).

Marx, K. (1844). Contribution to the critique of Hegel's Philosophy of Right: Introduction. In A. Ruge & K. Marx (Eds.), Deutsch-Französische Jahrbücher.

Marx, K. (1975). Critique of the Gotha Programme. In K. Marx & F. Engels, Selected works (Vol. 3) (E. V. Viana, Trans.). Editorial Progreso. (Original work written 1875, published 1891).

Marx, K. (1980). A contribution to the critique of political economy (J. Aricó, Trans.). Siglo XXI Editores. (Original work published 1859).

Marx, K. (2004). Economic and philosophical manuscripts of 1844 (F. Rubio Llorente, Trans.). Alianza Editorial. (Original work written 1844).

Marx, K., & Engels, F. (2012). The Communist Manifesto (P. Ribas, Trans.). Alianza Editorial. (Original work published 1848; 1888 edition with preface by F. Engels).

Netflix. 2017. What The Health. https://www.netflix.com/title/80174177.

Newland, C. (2022, May 8). Was Jesus an entrepreneur? https://empresa.org.ar/2022/fue-jesus-empresario/.

Nietzsche, F. (2000). The will to power (A. Ferrer, Trans.). Edaf. (Original work compilation 1901).

Nietzsche, F. (2003). On the genealogy of morality (J. L. López y L. de Lizaga, Trans.; D. Sánchez Meca, Ed.). Editorial Tecnos. (Original work published 1887).

Nietzsche, F. (2012). Thus spoke Zarathustra (J. L. Vermal, Trans.). Cátedra. (Original work published 1883-1885).

Spinoza, B. (2020). The Ethics–Ethica Ordine Geometrico Demonstrata (R.H.M. Elwes, Trans.). B&R Samizdat Express. (Original work published 1675).

Stalin, J. (1924). The foundations of Leninism. Editorial del Estado de Literatura Política.

Stalin, J. (1926). Questions of Leninism. Editorial del Estado de Literatura Política.

Wells, H.G. (1920). The outline of history [Kindle Edition]. Golden Classics.

Wikipedia, the free encyclopedia. en.wikipedia.org.

www.ingramcontent.com/pod-product-compliance
Lightning Source LLC
Chambersburg PA
CBHW072159160426
43197CB00012B/2453